Principles
in Practice

The Principles in Practice imprint offers teachers concrete illustrations of effective classroom practices based in NCTE research briefs and policy statements. Each book discusses the research on a specific topic, links the research to an NCTE brief or policy statement, and then demonstrates how those principles come alive in practice: by showcasing actual classroom practices that demonstrate the policies in action; by talking about research in practical, teacher-friendly language; and by offering teachers possibilities for rethinking their own practices in light of the ideas presented in the books. Books within the imprint are grouped in strands, each strand focused on a significant topic of interest.

Adolescent Literacy Strand

Adolescent Literacy at Risk? The Impact of Standards (2009) Rebecca Bowers Sipe

Adolescents and Digital Literacies: Learning Alongside Our Students (2010) Sara Kajder

Adolescent Literacy and the Teaching of Reading: Lessons for Teachers of Literature (2010) Deborah Appleman

Rethinking the "Adolescent" in Adolescent Literacy (2017) Sophia Tatiana Sarigianides, Robert Petrone, and Mark A. Lewis

Restorative Justice in the English Language Arts Classroom (2019) Maisha T. Winn, Hannah Graham, and Rita Renjitham Alfred

Writing in Today's Classrooms Strand

Writing in the Dialogical Classroom: Students and Teachers Responding to the Texts of Their Lives (2011) Bob Fecho

Becoming Writers in the Elementary Classroom: Visions and Decisions (2011) Katie Van Sluys

Writing Instruction in the Culturally Relevant Classroom (2011) Maisha T. Winn and Latrise P. Johnson

Literacy Assessment Strand

Our Better Judgment: Teacher Leadership for Writing Assessment (2012) Chris W. Gallagher and Eric D. Turley

Beyond Standardized Truth: Improving Teaching and Learning through Inquiry-Based Reading Assessment (2012) Scott Filkins

Reading Assessment: Artful Teachers, Successful Students (2013) Diane Stephens, editor

Going Public with Assessment: A Community Practice Approach (2018) Kathryn Mitchell Pierce and Rosario Ordoñez-Jasis

Literacies of the Disciplines Strand

Entering the Conversations: Practicing Literacy in the Disciplines (2014) Patricia Lambert Stock, Trace Schillinger, and Andrew Stock

Real-World Literacies: Disciplinary Teaching in the High School Classroom (2014) Heather Lattimer

Doing and Making Authentic Literacies (2014) Linda Denstaedt, Laura Jane Roop, and Stephen Best

Reading in Today's Classrooms Strand

Connected Reading: Teaching Adolescent Readers in a Digital World (2015) Kristen Hawley Turner and Troy Hicks

Digital Reading: What's Essential in Grades 3–8 (2015) William L. Bass II and Franki Sibberson

Teaching Reading with YA Literature: Complex Texts, Complex Lives (2016) Jennifer Buehler

Teaching English Language Learners Strand

Beyond "Teaching to the Test": Rethinking Accountability and Assessment for English Language Learners (2017) Betsy Gilliland and Shannon Pella

Community Literacies en Confianza: *Learning from Bilingual After-School Programs* (2017) Steven Alvarez

Understanding Language: Supporting ELL Students in Responsive ELA Classrooms (2017) Melinda McBee Orzulak

Writing across Culture and Language: Inclusive Strategies for Working with ELL Writers in the ELA Classroom (2017) Christina Ortmeier-Hooper

Restorative Justice in the English Language Arts Classroom

Maisha T. Winn
University of California, Davis

Hannah Graham
University of Wisconsin–Madison

Rita Renjitham Alfred
Restorative Justice Training Institute

National Council of Teachers of English
1111 W. Kenyon Road, Urbana, Illinois 61801-1096

Staff Editor: Bonny Graham

Imprint Editor: Cathy Fleischer

Interior Design: Victoria Pohlmann

Cover Design: Pat Mayer

Cover Images: upper left by The Parents Union / CC BY 2.0; upper right by the US Dept. of Education, CC BY; bottom left by Julie Mallozzi; bottom right a still from *Circle Up* by Julie Mallozzi

NCTE Stock Number: 41014; eStock Number: 41021

ISBN 978-0-8141-4101-4; eISBN 978-0-8141-4102-1

Library of Congress Cataloging-in-Publication Data

Names: Winn, Maisha T., author | Graham, Hannah, author. | Alfred, Rita Renjitham, 1955- author.

Title: Restorative justice in the English language arts classroom / Maisha T. Winn, Hannah Graham, Rita Renjitham Alfred.

Description: Urbana, Illinois : National Council of Teachers of English, [2019] | Includes bibliographical references and index.

Identifiers: LCCN 2019013927 (print) | LCCN 2019016181 (ebook) | ISBN 9780814141021 () | ISBN 9780814141014 (pbk) | ISBN 9780814141021 (E-ISBN)

Subjects: LCSH: Language arts—Social aspects—United States. | English language—Study and teaching—Social aspects—United States. | Youth with social disabilities—Education—United States. | Restorative justice—United States.

Classification: LCC LB1576 (ebook) | LCC LB1576 .W4897 2019 (print) | DDC 372.6—dc23

LC record available at https://lccn.loc.gov/2019013927

Contents

Prologue

In the summer of 2016, as we were writing this book, our efforts were often derailed by a seemingly endless barrage of violence echoing throughout the United States. Locally, Hannah and Maisha watched in horror as a video surfaced of an 18-year-old African American girl, Genele Laird, being beaten by two White police officers outside a shopping center in Madison, Wisconsin.[1] Less than two weeks later, all of us learned about Alton Sterling, an African American husband and father who was selling CDs outside a convenience store, being killed by police officers in Baton Rouge, Louisiana. This shooting was also captured on video, this time by the storeowner, who considered Mr. Sterling his friend. The very next day, we learned that another African American man, Philando Castile, who worked in the cafeteria of a Montessori school, was shot and killed by a Hispanic police officer who claimed to fear for his life. Mr. Castile's death was captured by his partner via Facebook Live as her 4-year-old daughter witnessed and consequently comforted her mother. Killings of police officers in Dallas, at the hands of a military-trained shooter, and Baton Rouge came next, and the United States was depicted as a "nation on the edge" by the media.[2] Fingers were pointed and guns were drawn as a debate on whose lives mattered ensued. In the fall of 2016, as we were completing this manuscript, we started waking up—once again—to more news of police shootings, including Terence Crutcher in Tulsa, Oklahoma, and Keith Lamont Scott, in Charlotte, North Carolina, launching more rebellions and exchanges between police and civilians. We couldn't forget the image of a police officer in a helicopter looking down at Mr. Crutcher and exclaiming that he looked like a "bad dude," which, we can only imagine, was a reference to his color (Black) and gender (male). There were some who pointed the finger westward to a multiracial San Francisco 49ers quarterback, Colin Kaepernick, who chose to kneel during "The Star Spangled Banner" in protest of police shooting and killing civilians. In between all the killings were verdicts of not guilty in other fatal incidents involving law enforcement and Black men and women.

Throughout all of this heartache, we—a team of educators, scholars, and restorative justice practitioners who proudly identify as Black (Maisha), Jewish (Hannah), and Southeast Asian (Rita)—kept thinking about the children. Picturing a 4-year-old child witnessing a man being shot and bleeding in the front seat of a car while she was in the backseat was unfathomable. Images of the 15-year-old son of Alton Sterling wailing at press conferences and his father's funeral were difficult to watch. We thought about these children who witnessed these events unfolding, as well as the aftermath, as they returned to school. As educators, we know that these children—and all children who are coming of age at this time—will have to overcome trauma to be engaged in learning. As scholars, we are all too familiar with research data demonstrating racial disparities in referrals, suspensions, and expulsions that mirror the criminal justice system on the streets and in the courts. And, finally, as restorative justice practitioners, products of the restorative justice process, and believers in the ability of restorative justice to build consensus and community, we understand that we have a lot of work to do to get these critical skills into the minds and practices of teachers in every classroom and every school across the country.

Who Are We and Why Are We Here?

Our paths crossed because we all care deeply about both children and the adults in school buildings who impart their wisdom, values, and lived experiences to these children, both implicitly and explicitly. Maisha, a language, literacy, and culture scholar with one foot firmly planted in English education, met Rita, a restorative justice practitioner and educator, through a leading restorative justice attorney and mutual friend, sujatha baliga,[3] who believed in our commitment to examining the intersectionality of restorative justice and education. Maisha was familiar with Rita's work with Cole Middle School and used a report documenting this work in her restorative English education training (Sumner, Silverman, & Frampton, 2010). Rita heard about Maisha's work in transforming ideas and talk into concrete artifacts that can be disseminated to induce cultural change. When Maisha and Rita first sat down together, Rita stated what should be obvious when we think about implementing restorative justice classrooms and schools but was not obvious to Maisha at the time: "I'm not into training kids. It's the adults who need training, not kids. Why should the kids carry the issues that are created by adults, for us? We are the ones who made this mess and now we have to fix this!"

Maisha and Hannah met at the University of Wisconsin–Madison, where Hannah was a graduate student and Maisha was the Susan J. Cellmer Distinguished Chair in Teacher Education and director of Secondary English, and in the early phases of creating a Restorative Justice English Education[4] project for preservice middle and high school English teachers. Hannah was interested in classroom talk and, prior to graduate school, had extensive experience developing curricula and working in teaching and learning spaces in both nonprofit and public school sectors in New York City, Tel Aviv, and Chicago. After learning about Hannah's experience as a teacher and curriculum developer, Maisha invited Hannah to join the Secondary English team, and they went on to co-teach the English Methods course and Hannah supervised student teachers, drawing from their experiences as classroom teachers in elementary and secondary environments.

Rita learned about restorative justice practices after many years of advocacy for youth of color using *social* and *transformative* justice philosophies, working to transform relationships in both the personal and the familial realms and in group, systems, and societal relationships, at both the macro and micro levels. Restorative justice, according to Rita, works relationally with power and invites everyone to speak their values to power by engaging in social issues that affect how people live. Restorative justice principles were present in the many social movements and struggles Rita learned about and has witnessed in her lifetime, such as the Montgomery boycott during the Civil Rights era and the end of apartheid in South Africa and that country's engagement in a truth and reconciliation process to "right" the "wrongs" of apartheid and the harm it caused.

We came to one another as stakeholders in classrooms and schools across the country. We agree that teachers need and deserve more support in building relationships with their students, but that these relationships should not function independently of their curricular choices. In our previous work with teachers, we found ourselves assembling materials from many different resources but wished there were a resource book that could serve as a road map for integrating restorative justice in the teaching of various subjects. This book is the outcome of our collective funds of knowledge, designed to share our experiences of and recommendations for teaching, writing, and learning restoratively.

What Do We Mean by Restorative Justice?

So what is this thing that people call "restorative justice"? At its core, restorative justice is a paradigm shift that seeks to make building and sustaining equitable relationships essential to everything we do. Yes, it is that simple. It is also one of the most powerful forms of accountability; through restorative justice processes—Circles, restorative case conferences, and conversations—stakeholders build consensus to right wrongs. In the context of the criminal justice system, restorative justice asks three simple questions: Who was harmed? What do they need? Whose obligations are these? These questions are a paradigm shift from our current criminal (retributive) justice system that privileges crime and punishment by asking: What is the crime? Who did it? What do they deserve? The former questions position the victim or the person or persons who have been harmed as agentive and deserving of having their harm addressed.

What does this have to do with classrooms and schools? The American criminal justice system permeates everything we do, especially in the ways most schools are currently constructed. Classrooms and schools have traditionally been (and continue to be) sites of punishment and systems of punishment, starting with early practices such as wearing dunce caps, sitting in the corner of the classroom, and even corporal punishment.[5] Isolation and even complete removal have become standard practices in classrooms and schools, which means children are missing precious time that should be devoted to learning, building intellectual curiosity, and finding platforms to amplify their ideas. In addition, a police presence is business as usual in many schools. Because it has become difficult in our education system to distinguish between the person who caused harm and the person who experienced harm, we contend that restorative justice is an opportunity and an invitation for teachers and students to address needs and obligations and to establish values that allow for a robust learning environment.

Reading This Book: An Overview

In bringing together our authorial voices, backgrounds, and beliefs, we are asking the same question posed to Mary Rose O'Reilley and her colleagues in Ihab Hassan's graduate seminar at the University of Wisconsin–Milwaukee, at the height of the Vietnam War—how do we teach English so that people stop killing? O'Reilley (1984) stated:

> My particular concern here is to explore the contribution we as teachers of writing and literature can make to "peace and world order studies," new curricula challenging our pose of moral neutrality on campuses across the country. Because my own "peace studies" course developed in the context of a traditional rhetoric program, I hope it will have something to say to our concerns about the relationship of classroom teaching to community values. (p. 103)

While elsewhere Maisha has asked how math, social studies, and science (in addition to English) might be taught in a way that helps people to stop killing (Winn, 2016), in this book we focus on the English language arts classroom: how it can be transformed into a deliberate, equitable, and thoughtful "change lab" using writing and reading techniques that inspire empathy, discussion, and social action, providing opportunities for teachers and their students to engage in a restorative English education. Although we offer suggested practices, anecdotes from teachers, and curricular concepts focused on how to engage in a restorative English education throughout this book, the work of restoration is at its core about *mindset*; it is not a convenient program or list of best practices. All adults working with children have to engage in the difficult work of retraining their minds to be more critical of their own biases and finding tangible ways to exchange this bias for true understanding and valuing of fellow human beings. This book reflects the interwoven importance of educator mindset and classroom technique in illuminating the qualities of a restorative English language arts classroom. Chapters offer windows into restorative philosophies, future reading lists, and pedagogic practices in the following order:

> Chapter 1: Brings the need for a restorative English education into focus and articulates its alignment with the NCTE literacy brief on adolescent literacy.
>
> Chapter 2: Offers a history of restorative justice in education and gives an overview of the power of Circles in redressing harm and creating community.
>
> Chapter 3: Offers specific ways that ELA teachers can approach their curriculum and pedagogy to create a restorative English educative space.
>
> Chapter 4: Provides the means for educators to assess themselves and their classrooms in the context of restorative justice principles.
>
> Chapter 5: Outlines next steps and provides specific, concrete examples of how teachers and teaching teams can continue this work beyond this book.

The following chapters provide a road map for how English teachers can significantly engage in the work of integrating restorative principles into their classrooms. We fear this work will sound ephemeral; however, given the current climate of violence against Black and Brown people and the sparring between #BlackLivesMatter and #AllLivesMatter, it is time to do transformational work, starting with the English classroom and using the tools that have influenced the thinking and actions of others. ELA teachers have the opportunity to work with mediums of literacy that can be transformative for their students and themselves; this book seeks to support this work.

Honoring and Remembering Historical Roots

Finally, and before we can go any further, we want to ask permission from and offer respect and honor to the Indigenous peoples from whom restorative justice practices originated, including the Ohlone people and the Patwin/Wintu/Wintun tribes, whose land Maisha and Rita now live on in California. We also offer respect and honor to the Dakota Sioux, Ho-chunk, Menominee, Ojibwe, Potawatomi, and Fox and Sauk tribes, whose land Hannah lives on in Wisconsin. We are grateful for their generosity and to Rita's lineage of teachers in restorative justice—the Tagish and Tlingit First Nations people from the Yukon, Canada—who brought the restorative justice practice called "Peacemaking Circles" to us in the United States. The First Nations people and the First Peoples in many parts of the world have practiced this way of being with their communities, handled issues of hurt and harm using these practices, and continue to use these practices even in the face of continued colonization and state-sanctioned violence, as in North Dakota, where they are fighting (resisting) the Dakota Access Pipeline. Recognizing the history of cultural and physical appropriation and colonization of Indigenous peoples may feel both overwhelming and necessary, especially because RJ scholars and educators have moved away from acknowledging the historical context of our work.

An Invitation

This book is an opportunity and invitation to find ways to create a literacy classroom that prioritizes relationships. We believe that when relationships are prioritized, learning will happen. We also believe that creating the foundation for relationships is just the beginning. This book can serve as a guide and a first step in this important work; however, it cannot and must not take the place of engaging in restorative justice Circle Keeper training, which we encourage all readers of this book to complete.[6] We hope you will join us on this journey to rethinking our classroom spaces—and the ELA classroom in particular—as the site for healing and moving forward.

Welcome.

Adolescent Literacy
An NCTE Policy Research Brief

Causes for Concern

It is easy to summon the language of crisis in discussing adolescent literacy. After all, a recent study of writing instruction reveals that 40 percent of high school seniors never or rarely write a paper of three or more pages, and although 4th and 8th graders showed some improvement in writing between 1998 and 2002, the scores of 12th graders showed no significant change. Less than half of the 2005 ACT-tested high school graduates demonstrated readiness for college-level reading, and the 2005 National Assessment of Educational Progress (NAEP) reading scores for 12th graders showed a decrease from 80 percent at the *proficient* level in 1992 to 73 percent in 2005.

Recent NAEP results also reveal a persistent achievement gap between the reading and writing scores of whites and students of color in 8th and 12th grades. Furthermore, both whites and students of color scored lower in reading in 2005 as compared with 1992, and both male and female students also scored lower in 2005.[1]

The challenges associated with adolescent literacy extend beyond secondary school to both college and elementary school. Many elementary school teachers worry about the 4th-grade slump in reading abilities. Furthermore, preliminary analysis of reading instruction in the elementary school suggests that an emphasis on processes of how to read can crowd out attention to reading for ideas, information, and concepts—the very skills adolescents need to succeed in secondary school. In the other direction, college instructors claim that students arrive in their classes ill-prepared to take up the literacy tasks of higher education, and employers lament the inadequate literacy skills of young workers. In our increasingly "flat" world, the U.S. share of the global college-educated workforce has fallen from 30 percent to 14 percent in recent decades as young workers in developing nations demonstrate employer-satisfying proficiency in literacy.[2]

In this context, many individuals and groups, including elected officials, governmental entities, foundations, and media outlets—some with little knowledge of the field—have stepped forward to shape policies that impact literacy instruction. Notably, the U.S. Congress is currently discussing new Striving Readers legislation (Bills S958 and HR2289) designed to improve the literacy skills of middle and high school students. Test scores and other numbers do not convey the full complexity of literacy even though they are effective in eliciting a feeling of crisis. Accordingly, a useful alternative would be for teachers and other informed professionals to take an interest in policy that shapes literacy instruction. This document provides research-based information to support that interest.

Common Myths about Adolescent Literacy

Myth: Literacy refers only to reading.

Reality: Literacy encompasses reading, writing, and a variety of social and intellectual practices that call upon the voice as well as the eye and hand. It also extends to new media—including nondigitized multimedia, digitized multimedia, and hypertext or hypermedia.[3]

Adolescent Literacy

Myth: Students learn everything about reading and writing in elementary school.

Reality: Some people see the processes of learning to read and write as similar to learning to ride a bicycle, as a set of skills that do not need further development once they have been achieved. Actually literacy learning is an ongoing and nonhierarchical process. Unlike math where one principle builds on another, literacy learning is recursive and requires continuing development and practice.[4]

Myth: Literacy instruction is the responsibility of English teachers alone.

Reality: Each academic content area poses its own literacy challenges in terms of vocabulary, concepts, and topics. Accordingly, adolescents in secondary school classes need explicit instruction in the literacies of each discipline as well as the actual content of the course so that they can become successful readers and writers in all subject areas.[5]

Myth: Academics are all that matter in literacy learning.

Reality: Research shows that out-of-school literacies play a very important role in literacy learning, and teachers can draw on these skills to foster learning in school. Adolescents rely on literacy in their identity development, using reading and writing to define themselves as persons. The discourses of specific disciplines and social/cultural contexts created by school classrooms shape the literacy learning of adolescents, especially when these discourses are different and conflicting.[6]

Myth: Students who struggle with one literacy will have difficulty with all literacies.

Reality: Even casual observation shows that students who struggle with reading a physics text may be excellent readers of poetry; the student who has difficulty with word problems in math may be very comfortable with historical narratives. More important, many of the literacies of adolescents are largely invisible in the classroom. Research on reading and writing beyond the classroom shows that students often have literacy skills that are not made evident in the classroom unless teachers make special efforts to include them.[7]

Myth: School writing is essentially an assessment tool that enables students to show what they have learned.

Reality: While it is true that writing is often central to assessment of what students have learned in school, it is also a means by which students learn and develop. Research shows that informal writing to learn can help increase student learning of content material, and it can even improve the summative writing in which students show what they have learned.[8]

Understanding Adolescent Literacy

Overview: Dimensions of Adolescent Literacy

In adolescence, students simultaneously begin to develop important literacy resources and experience unique literacy challenges. By fourth grade many students have learned a number of the basic processes of reading and writing; however, they still need to master literacy practices unique to different levels, disciplines, texts, and situations. As adolescents experience the shift to content-area learning, they need help from teachers to develop the confidence and skills necessary for specialized academic literacies.

Adolescents also begin to develop new literacy resources and participate in multiple discourse communities in and out of school. Frequently students' extracurricular literacy proficiencies are not valued in school. Literacy's link to community and identity means that it can be a site of resistance for adolescents. When students are not recognized for bringing valuable, multiple-literacy practices to school, they can become resistant to school-based literacy.[9]

1. Shifting Literacy Demands

The move from elementary to secondary school entails many changes including fundamental ones in the nature of literacy requirements. For adolescents, school-based literacy shifts as students engage with disciplinary content and a wide variety of difficult texts and writing tasks. Elementary school usually prepares students in the processes of reading, but many adolescents do not understand the multiple dimensions of content-based literacies. Adolescents may struggle with reading in some areas and do quite well with others. They may also be challenged to write in ways that conform to new disciplinary discourses. The proliferation of high-stakes tests can complicate the literacy learning of adolescents, particularly if test preparation takes priority over content-specific literacy instruction across the disciplines.[10]

Research says . . .

- Adolescents are less likely to struggle when subject area teachers make the reading and writing approaches in a given content area clear and visible.
- Writing prompts in which students reflect on their current understandings, questions, and learning processes help to improve content-area learning.[11]
- Effective teachers model how they access specific content-area texts.
- Learning the literacies of a given discipline can help adolescents negotiate multiple, complex discourses and recognize that texts can mean different things in different contexts.
- Efficacious teaching of cross-disciplinary literacies has a social justice dimension as well as an intellectual one.[12]

2. Multiple and Social Literacies

Adolescent literacy is social, drawing from various discourse communities in and out of school. Adolescents already have access to many different discourses including those of ethnic, online, and popular culture communities. They regularly use literacies for social and political purposes as they create meanings and participate in shaping their immediate environments.[13]

Teachers often devalue, ignore, or censor adolescents' extracurricular literacies, assuming that these literacies are morally suspect, raise controversial issues, or distract adolescents from more important work. This means that some adolescents' literacy abilities remain largely invisible in the classroom.[14]

Adolescent Literacy

Research says . . .

- The literacies adolescents bring to school are valuable resources, but they should not be reduced to stereotypical assumptions about predictable responses from specific populations of students.
- Adolescents are successful when they understand that texts are written in social settings and for social purposes.
- Adolescents need bridges between everyday literacy practices and classroom communities, including online, non-book-based communities.
- Effective teachers understand the importance of adolescents finding enjoyable texts and don't always try to shift students to "better" books.[15]

3. Importance of Motivation

Motivation can determine whether adolescents engage with or disengage from literacy learning. If they are not engaged, adolescents with strong literacy skills may choose not to read or write. The number of students who are not engaged with or motivated by school learning grows at every grade level, reaching epidemic proportions in high school. At the secondary level, students need to build confidence to meet new literacy challenges because confident readers are more likely to be engaged. Engagement is encouraged through meaningful connections.[16]

Research says . . .

Engaged adolescents demonstrate internal motivation, self-efficacy, and a desire for mastery. Providing student choice and responsive classroom environments with connections to "real life" experiences helps adolescents build confidence and stay engaged.[17]

A. Student Choice

- Self-selection and variety engage students by enabling ownership in literacy activities.
- In adolescence, book selection options increase dramatically, and successful readers need to learn to choose texts they enjoy. If they can't identify pleasurable books, adolescents often lose interest in reading.
- Allowing student choice in writing tasks and genres can improve motivation. At the same time, writing choice must be balanced with a recognition that adolescents also need to learn the literacy practices that will support academic success.
- Choice should be meaningful. Reading materials should be appropriate and should speak to adolescents' diverse interests and varying abilities.
- Student-chosen tasks must be supported with appropriate instructional support or scaffolding.[18]

B. Responsive Classroom Environments

- Caring, responsive classroom environments enable students to take ownership of literacy activities and can counteract negative emotions that lead to lack of motivation.
- Instruction should center around learners. Active, inquiry-based activities engage reluctant academic readers and writers. Inquiry-based writing connects writing practices with real-world experiences and tasks.

- Experiences with task-mastery enable increased self-efficacy, which leads to continued engagement.
- Demystifying academic literacy helps adolescents stay engaged.
- Using technology is one way to provide learner-centered, relevant activities. For example, many students who use computers to write show more engagement and motivation and produce longer and better papers.
- Sustained experiences with diverse texts in a variety of genres that offer multiple perspectives on life experiences can enhance motivation, particularly if texts include electronic and visual media.[19]

4. Value of Multicultural Perspectives

Monocultural approaches to teaching can cause or increase the achievement gap and adolescents' disengagement with literacy. Students should see value in their own cultures and the cultures of others in their classrooms. Students who do not find representations of their own cultures in texts are likely to lose interest in school-based literacies. Similarly, they should see their home languages as having value. Those whose home language is devalued in the classroom will usually find school less engaging.

Research says . . .
Multicultural literacy is seeing, thinking, reading, writing, listening, and discussing in ways that critically confront and bridge social, cultural, and personal differences. It goes beyond a "tourist" view of cultures and encourages engagement with cultural issues in all literature, in all classrooms, and in the world.[20]

A. Multicultural Literacy across All Classrooms

- Multicultural education does not by itself foster cultural inclusiveness because it can sometimes reinforce stereotypical perceptions that need to be addressed critically.
- Multicultural literacy is not just a way of reading "ethnic" texts or discussing issues of "diversity," but rather is a holistic way of *being* that fosters social responsibility and extends well beyond English/language arts classrooms.
- Teachers need to acknowledge that we all have cultural frameworks within which we operate, and everyone—teachers and students alike—needs to consider how these frameworks can be challenged or changed to benefit all peoples.[21]
- Teacher knowledge of social science, pedagogical, and subject-matter content knowledge about diversity will foster adolescents' learning.
- Successful literacy development among English language learners depends on and fosters collaborative multicultural relationships among researchers, teachers, parents, and students.
- Integration of technology will enhance multicultural literacy.
- Confronting issues of race and ethnicity within classrooms and in the larger community will enhance student learning and engagement.[22]

B. Goals of Multicultural Literacy

- Students will view knowledge from diverse ethnic and cultural perspectives, and use knowledge to guide action that will create a humane and just world.
- Teachers will help students understand the whiteness studies principle that white is a race so they can develop a critical perspective on racial thinking by people of all skin colors.
- Multicultural literacy will serve as a means to move between cultures and communities and develop transnational understandings and collaboration.
- Ideally, students will master basic literacies *and* become multiculturally literate citizens who foster a democratic multicultural society.[23]

Research-Based Recommendations for Effective Adolescent Literacy Instruction

For teachers . . .

Research on the practices of highly effective adolescent literacy teachers reveals a number of common qualities. Teachers who have received recognition for their classroom work, who are typically identified as outstanding by their peers and supervisors, and whose students consistently do well on high-stakes tests share a number of qualities. These qualities, in order of importance, include the following:

1. teaching with approaches that foster critical thinking, questioning, student decision-making, and independent learning;
2. addressing the diverse needs of adolescents whose literacy abilities vary considerably;
3. possessing personal characteristics such as caring about students, being creative and collaborative, and loving to read and write;
4. developing a solid knowledge about and commitment to literacy instruction;
5. using significant quality and quantity of literacy activities including hands-on, scaffolding, mini-lessons, discussions, group work, student choice, ample feedback, and multiple forms of expression;
6. participating in ongoing professional development;
7. developing quality relationships with students; and
8. managing the classroom effectively.[24]

For school programs . . .

Research on successful school programs for adolescent literacy reveals fifteen features that contribute to student achievement:

1. direct and explicit instruction;
2. effective instructional principles embedded in content;
3. motivation and self-directed learning;
4. text-based collaborative learning;

5. strategic tutoring;

6. diverse texts;

7. intensive writing;

8. technology;

9. ongoing formative assessment of students;

10. extended time for literacy;

11. long-term and continuous professional development, especially that provided by literacy coaches;

12. ongoing summative assessment of students and programs;

13. interdisciplinary teacher teams;

14. informed administrative and teacher leadership; and

15. comprehensive and coordinated literacy program.[25]

For policymakers . . .

A national survey produced action steps for policymakers interested in fostering adolescent literacy. These include:

1. align the high school curriculum with postsecondary expectations so that students are well prepared for college;

2. focus state standards on the essentials for college and work readiness;

3. shape high school courses to conform with state standards;

4. establish core course requirements for high school graduation;

5. emphasize higher-level reading skills across the high school curriculum;

6. make sure students attain the skills necessary for effective writing;

7. ensure that students learn science process and inquiry skills; and

8. monitor and share information about student progress.[26]

This report is produced by NCTE's James R. Squire Office of Policy Research, directed by Anne Ruggles Gere, with assistance from Laura Aull, Hannah Dickinson, Melinda McBee Orzulak, and Ebony Elizabeth Thomas, all students in the Joint PhD Program in English and Education at the University of Michigan.

Notes

1. ACT. (2006). *Aligning postsecondary expectations and high school practice: The gap defined: Policy implications of the ACT national curriculum survey results 2005–2006.* Iowa City, IA. Retrieved on July 3, 2007, from http://www.act.org/path/policy/pdf/NationalCurriculum Survey2006.pdf

Applebee, A., & Langer, J. (2006). *The state of writing instruction in America's schools: What existing data tell us.* Center on English Learning and Achievement. Retrieved on July 3, 2007, from http://cela.albany.edu

Adolescent Literacy

National Center for Education Statistics. (2002). *National Assessment of Educational Progress (NAEP). NAEP Writing–Average writing scale score results, grades 4, 8, and 12: 1998 and 2002*. Retrieved on July 3, 2007, from http://nces.ed.gov/nationsreportcard/writing/results2002/natscalescore.asp

National Center for Education Statistics. (2006). *National Assessment of Educational Progress (NAEP). Reading Results: Executive Summary for Grades 4 and 8*. Retrieved on July 3, 2007, from http://nces.ed.gov/nationsreportcard/reading/

2. Altwerger, B., Arya, P., Jin, L., Jordan, N. L., et al. (2004). When research and mandates collide: The challenges and dilemmas of teacher education in the era of NCLB. *English Education, 36*, 119–133.

National Center on Education and the Economy. (2007). *Tough choices or tough times: The report of the New Commission on the Skills of the American Workforce*. San Francisco, CA: Jossey-Bass.

3. Brandt, D. (2001). *Literacy in American lives*. New York: Cambridge University Press.

Gee, J. (2007). *Social linguistics and literacies: Ideology in discourses*. London: Taylor & Francis.

4. Franzak, J. K. (2006). *Zoom*. A review of the literature on marginalized adolescent readers, literacy theory, and policy implications. *Review of Educational Research, 76*(2), 209–248.

5. Sturtevant, E., & Linek, W. (2003). The instructional beliefs and decisions of middle and secondary teachers who successfully blend literacy and content. *Reading Research & Instruction, 43*, 74–90.

6. Guzzetti, B., & Gamboa, M. (2004). 'Zines for social justice: Adolescent girls writing on their own. *Reading Research Quarterly, 39*, 408–437.

Langer, J. (2001). Beating the odds: Teaching middle and high school students to read and write well. *American Educational Research Journal, 38*(4), 837–880.

Nielsen, L. (2006). Playing for real: Texts and the performance of identity. In D. Alvermann, K. Hinchman, D. Moore, S. Phelps, & D. Waff (Eds.), *Reconceptualizing the literacies in adolescents' lives* (2nd ed.) Mahwah, NJ: Lawrence Erlbaum, 5–28.

Sturtevant, E. & Linek, W. (2003).

7. Moje, E. B. (2002). Re-framing adolescent literacy research for new times: Studying youth as a resource. *Reading Research and Instruction, 41*, 211–228.

8. Boscolo, P., & Mason, L. (2001). Writing to learn, writing to transfer. In G. Jijlaarsdam, P. Tynjala, L. Mason, & K. Londa (Eds.), *Studies in writing: Vol 7. Writing as a learning tool: Integrating theory and practice*. Dordrecht, The Netherlands: Kluwer Academic Publishers, 83–104.

9. Lenters, K. (2006). Resistance, struggle, and the adolescent reader. *Journal of Adolescent and Adult Literacy, 50*(2), 136–142.

10. Moje, E. B., & Sutherland, L. M. (2003). The future of middle school literacy education. *English Education, 35*(2), 149–164.

Snow, C. E., & Biancarosa, G. (2003). *Adolescent literacy and the achievement: What do we know and where do we go from here?* New York: Carnegie Corporation. Retrieved June 23, 2007, from http://www.all4ed.org/resources/CarnegieAdolescentLiteracyReport.pdf

11. Bangert-Drowns, R. L., Hurley, M. M., & Wilkinson, B. (2004). The effects of school-based writing-to-learn interventions on academic achievement: A meta-analysis. *Review of Educational Research, 74*, 29–58.

Greenleaf, C. L., Schoenbach, R., Cziko, C., & Mueller, F. (2001). Apprenticing adolescent readers to academic literacy. *Harvard Education Review, 71*(1), 79–129.

12. Moje, E. B., Ciechanowski, K. M., Kramer, K., Ellis, L., Carrillo, R., & Collazo, T. (2004). Working toward third space in content area literacy: An examination of everyday funds of knowledge and discourse. *Reading Research Quarterly, 39*(1), 38–70.

13. Moje, E. B. (2007). Developing socially just subject-matter instruction: A review of the literature on disciplinary literacy. N. L. Parker (Ed.), *Review of research in education.* (pp. 1–44). Washington, DC: American Educational Research Association.

14. Kim, J. L. W., & Monique, L. (2004). Pleasure reading: Associations between young women's sexual attitudes and their reading of contemporary women's magazines. *Psychology of Women Quarterly, 28*(1), 48–58.

Kliewer, C., Biklen, D., & Kasa-Hendrickson, C. (2006). Who may be literate? Disability and resistance to the cultural denial of competence. *American Educational Research Journal, 43*(2), 163–192.

Moje, E. B., & Sutherland, L. M. (2003).

15. Moje, E. B. (2007).

Ross, C. S. (2001). Making choices: What readers say about choosing books for pleasure. In W. Katz (Ed.), *Reading, Books, and Librarians.* New York: Haworth Information Press.

16. Guthrie, J. T., Van Meter, P., McCann, A. D., Wigfield, A., Bennett, L., & Poundstone, C. C. (1996). Growth of literacy engagement: Changes in motivations and strategies during concept-oriented reading instruction. *Reading Research Quarterly, 31*, 306–332.

17. Guthrie, J. T. (2001). Contexts for engagement and motivation in reading. *Reading Online.* International Reading Association. Retrieved June 23, 2007, from http://www.readingonline.org/articles/handbook/guthrie/index.html

Guthrie, J. T., & Humenick, N. M. (2004). Motivating students to read: Evidence for classroom practices that increase reading motivation and achievement. In P. McCardle and V. Chhabra (Eds.), *The voice of evidence in reading research.* Baltimore, MD: Brookes, 329–354.

18. Biancarosa, G., & Snow, C. (2004). *Reading next: A vision for action and research in*

Adolescent Literacy

middle and high school literacy. Report to Carnegie Corporation of New York. Washington, DC: Alliance for Excellent Education. Retrieved June 25, 2007, from http://www.all4ed.org/publications/ReadingNext/ReadingNext.pdf

Guthrie, J. T. (2001).

Oldfather, P. (1994). *When students do not feel motivated for literacy learning: How a responsive classroom culture helps.* College Park, MD: University of Maryland, National Reading Research Center. Retrieved June 25, 2007, from http://curry.edschool.virginia.edu/go/clic/nrrc/rspon_r8.html; NCREL (2005).

19. Goldberg, A., Russell, M., & Cook, A. (2003). The effects of computers on student writing: A meta-analysis of studies from 1992 to 2002. *Journal of Technology, Learning, and Assessment, 2*, 1–51.

Greenleaf et al. (2001).

Guthrie, J. T. (2001).

Kamil, M. (2003).

Ray, K. W. (2006). Exploring inquiry as a teaching stance in the writing workshop. *Language Arts, 83*(3), 238–248.

20. Cai, M. (1998). Multiple definitions of multicultural literature: Is the debate really just "ivory tower" bickering? *New Advocate, 11*(4), 11–24.

Hade, D. (1997). Reading multiculturally. In V. Harris (Ed.), *Using multi-ethnic literature in the K–8 classroom.* Norwood: Christopher-Gordon.

Taxel, J. (1992). The politics of children's literature: Reflections on multiculturalism, political correctness, and Christopher Columbus. In V. Harris (Ed.), *Teaching multicultural literature in grades K–8.* Norwood: Christopher-Gordon.

21. Fang, Z., Fu, D., & Lamme, L. (1999). Rethinking the role of multicultural literature in literacy instruction: Problems, paradox, and possibilities. *New Advocate, 12*(3), 259–276.

Nieto, S. (2000). *Affirming diversity: The sociopolitical context of multicultural education.* New York: Longman.

Rochman, H. (1993). Beyond political correctness. In D. Fox & K. Short (Eds.), *Stories matter: The complexity of cultural authenticity in children's literature.* Urbana: NCTE.

Taxel, J. (1992).

22. Banks, J. A. (1991). Teaching multicultural literacy to teachers. *Teaching Education, 4*(1), 135–144.

Diamond, B. J., & Moore, M. A. (1995). Multicultural literacy: Mirroring the reality of the classroom. New York: Longman.

Feuerverger, G. (1994). A multicultural literacy intervention for minority language students. *Language and Education, 8*(3), 123–146.

Freedman, S. W. (1999). *Inside city schools: Investigating literacy in multicultural classrooms.* New York: Teachers College Press.

23. Banks, J. A. (2004). *Handbook of research on multicultural education*. San Francisco: Jossey-Bass.

Jay, G. S. (2005). Whiteness studies and the multicultural literature classroom. *MELUS, 30*(2), 99–121.

Luke, A., & Carpenter, M. (2003). Literacy education for a new ethics of global community. *Language Arts, 81*(1), 20.

24. Applebee, A., Langer, J., Nystrand, M., & Gamoran, A. (2003). Discussion-based approaches to developing understanding: Classroom instruction and student performance in middle and high school English. *American Educational Research Journal, 40*, 685–730.

Paris, S. R., & Block, C. C. (2007). The expertise of adolescent literacy teachers. *Journal of Adolescent & Adult Literacy, 50*(7), 582–596.

25. Biancarosa, G., & Snow, C. E. (2004).

26. ACT, 2006.

This publication of the James R. Squire Office of Policy Research offers updates on research with implications for policy decisions that affect teaching and learning. Each issue addresses a different topic. Download this issue at http://www.ncte.org/about/over/positions/category/literacy/127676.htm. Read more on this topic at http://www.ncte.org/pubs/chron/highlights/127825.htm.

Teaching English in the Age of Mass Incarceration

W e begin our discussion of restorative justice with the questions that drive our work: Why should English teachers have to think about the impact of mass incarceration and unequal treatment that we raised in the preface? Why must we concern ourselves with the realities of criminalization that strike hardest the poor, Black, Latinx, Indigenous, LGBTQIPA+, differently abled, and other minoritized[7] children in our schools? As an English teacher, you might be wondering about the connections we see—because isn't the ELA classroom a space where teachers can use writing and reading to visit imagined worlds? All three of us (and we imagine many of you as well) have used literature to catapult us into another time, space, or experience, and, perhaps, to escape challenges in our lives. Maisha recalls getting lost as a child in the L. Frank Baum Wizard of Oz series, marveling over the fact that a series that focuses on various characters such as Ozma, The Patchwork Girl, and Rinkitink preceded the widely adored film. Hannah spent many hours engrossed in J. R. R. Tolkien's *The Hobbit,* captivated by the alternate universe Tolkien's fantastical characters inhabited. Rita's love for poetry—including poets from her native Singapore such as Chandran Nair, Lee Tzu Pheng, and Kirpal Singh, and Ugandan Theo Luzuka—connected her to longing for home. Rita recalls spending time with Rumi, grasshoppers and geese with Mary Oliver, and soulful, quiet moments with Richard Wagamese. Reading and writing was a way for Rita to enjoy and commune with friends and family.

As former English language arts teachers, Hannah and Maisha built on those memories, using expository and creative techniques to transport students into new paradigms that drew on imagined worlds through persuasive writing and imagining/writing themselves in the role of a character. In doing so, we asked students to use different lenses and consider perspectives other than their own, not as an effort to dismiss their individual and collective truths, but rather as an opportunity to practice empathy.

But beyond the use of imaginative literature, we also facilitated opportunities to engage students in thinking about race, class, gender, and privilege using reading and writing as tools for exploring the nuances of humanity, relationships, and place (Winn & Johnson, 2011). Now more than ever, we believe English teachers need to provide space in their classrooms for examining and critiquing society. In a time when racial tumult and assaults against LGBTQIPA+ peoples are being captured on cell phones and witnessed in ways that make it difficult to turn away or avoid discussions about racism, implicit bias, classism, and discrimination, it is necessary to reimagine the ELA classroom as a place to practice justice. One crucial component of practicing justice in today's schools and classrooms is being deliberate about addressing mass incarceration, what Alexander (2010) refers to as the most pressing civil rights issue of the twenty-first century. In doing so, ELA teachers have the opportunity to teach in ways that are humanizing, restorative, relevant, and sustaining.

This book is a beginning guide for ELA teachers looking to address harm and inequities in their classroom, school, and community. Elsewhere, Maisha has asked, What are conversations about jails, prisons, and isolation doing in a nice place like the ELA classroom (Winn, 2011)? In this chapter, we continue that conversation as we address the following questions:

- Why should ELA teachers care about mass incarceration and the criminalization of particular youth?
- What should teachers know about this phenomenon in connection with schooling and literacy?
- What resources support teachers who want to learn more about and challenge the discrimination against and criminalization of minoritized students?

Additionally, this chapter illuminates the relationship between restorative justice in the ELA classroom and *Adolescent Literacy: An NCTE Policy Research Brief.* This brief sets forth four dimensions of adolescent literacy: (1) shifting literacy demands; (2) multiple and social literacies; (3) the importance of motivation; and (4) the value of a multicultural perspective. Viewing these dimensions of adolescent literacy through a restorative justice lens leads us to recognize just how integral practicing empathy and justice is to developing adolescent literacy.

Why Should We (ELA Teachers) Care?

The culture of mass incarceration—and, more specifically, the pervasiveness of the criminalization of particular children—impacts everyone (Morris, 2016; Coates, 2015). Having access to literacy or even being considered literate comes with privileges, whereas those who are perceived as illiterate, as inarticulate, or as struggling readers and writers are often relegated to a second-class citizenship in both school and out-of-school spaces. All too often, struggling learners get typecast as problems and even as potential criminals. Acknowledging America's dubious history of literacy and the ways in which literacy was legislated away from enslaved Africans (Gilyard, 1996) is an important first step for literacy teachers in general, and especially for those who work with minoritized youth. However, simply knowing this is not enough. Giving only a brief nod to this time and place in history creates a deficit narrative that continues to hold Black children, their families, and their teachers captive. Understanding more deeply the intersections of race, class, language, and inequality is key to not perpetuating historic and chronic inequality in the classroom. Alim (2016) argues that race and language must be analyzed together in order to understand the relationship between race, language, and power. *Raciolinguistics*—a term coined by Alim—serves as an intersection for the historical context of words and language, as well as for contemporary understandings of how words and language get assigned to race in potentially dehumanizing ways.

Practically, what does this mean for you as a reader of this book? Teachers—and English teachers especially—stand in the aftermath of these debates about language, including debates about what counts as "Standard" and whose language counts as legitimate and, thus, is deemed worthy to be spoken in classroom contexts. English teachers are often unaware of their own implicit biases that frame particular children and their families as sounding or seeming un- or undereducated. Scholar Keith Gilyard (1996) moves beyond explaining African Americans' tenuous history with the English language by suggesting that we also "flip the script," outlining how people of African descent have been agentive with language by creating opportunities to own a language that was not intended for them to acquire. In other words, how is it that a community of people for whom literacy in a Western context was out of reach were able to not only learn to read and write but also find ways to make the language their own through writing, speaking, and

Resource Spotlight

Gilyard, K. (1996). *Let's Flip the Script: An African American Discourse on Language, Literature, and Learning.* Detroit, MI: Wayne State University Press.

Why teachers should read this work:

- In a series of essays, Gilyard provides a critical overview of African Americans and language in the context of the United States.

- Gilyard masterfully reframes the narrative of African American literate practices in ways that disrupt the monolithic view of African American people's language use as solely oral.

doing? Gilyard argues that people of African descent "flipped the script"—borrowing the phrase from the youth who use it as a way to acknowledge the ingenuity of their peers. Flipping the script, in this sense, acknowledges the myriad ways young people are agentive with language and often create their own space if one isn't readily available—just as their ancestors did.

Another way to flip the script involves recognizing and integrating positive images of minoritized readers and writers. Maisha's study of Black bookstores as "supplementary" and "alternative" knowledge spaces demonstrates the importance of this. Her work includes interviews with Black writers, poets, and parents who used Black bookstore events either as part of their extended curriculum as homeschoolers or to bolster the learning (or lack thereof) taking place in their children's schools (Fisher, 2006, 2009; Winn, 2016). A theme throughout the study is that parents of Black children want to expose their children to these positive images of Black readers and writers that they felt were omitted in English classrooms:

> I always take my children with me, if I can, to listen, to meet black leaders and black writers especially. I always do. I've always done it because they're not going to get that in school and by being inundated with the media and other [negative] images. So I want them to have images—literary images of Black people who can read and write and think. So I take them [because] I want them to know our [stories]. I want them to know *our* stories from *our* perspectives. (Mrs. Shabazz, parent participant at Carol's Books and Marcus Books, qtd. in Fisher, 2006)

Keeping in mind this notion of flipping the script, we recommend that English teachers consider engaging in a sociocritical literacy—a literacy that, according to Gutiérrez (2008a, 2008b), privileges historicizing the lives of *all* students and, we would add, the lives of teachers (a curricular objective we also further explore in Chapters 3 and 4 of this book). Historicizing one's life entails examining the practices and traditions of language in connection with the literate practices we use. Why is this important for teachers in particular? Because reaching an awareness of our particular practices can help us resist normalizing ourselves or thinking that our ways of learning and being are the standard to which all students should aspire.

One Example of Teacher Practice

How might we begin to engage in historicizing practices with our students? Consider one of Maisha's favorite writing activities, the "I am from" poem, a strategy that invites students to historicize their lives, name the lived experiences of their families and loved ones, and use writing as a way to map their contributions to the world. "I am from" poems begin with listing words and images from students' lives, such as names found in the family, family traditions, food items, relatives, and more—including a category for "sayings/proverbs/words of wisdom" heard in one's family. To honor the multiple experiences and languages of her students, Maisha always invites them to write their words and images in their first language. Mapping out these responses on poster paper throughout a classroom reminds everyone in the room that they are part of something larger, and that everyone has a story.

When Maisha was a professor at Emory University directing the Secondary English program, she introduced the "I am from" poem to her students (preservice and practicing teachers) the first week of the English Methods course. Subsequently, all of her students used this scaffold with their own students, and one of Maisha's student teachers even started a phenomenon at the middle school where she was working: students shared their poems with their peers, and soon other students in the school building asked their teachers if they could write one too.

What was it about having students write these poems and share "their stories" from "their perspectives"—to borrow the words from Mrs. Shabazz, a participant in Maisha's dissertation research—that motivated them to write? The "I am from" poem moves beyond merely celebrating differences to give students and teachers an opportunity to see the nuances in family traditions, and it also supports White students who see themselves as void of "culture" in understanding that they too have experiences that are unique to their families and communities.

A coda to this story is that one of the other teachers in this middle school informed the student teacher that the "I am from" activity was "exciting" the students "too much," and she planned to retreat to a more rote method of teaching writing that ensured students would sit at their desks and be quiet. This endnote to a story of enthusiastic student literacy is an example of the pushback against historicizing the lives of our students. Why was this teacher fearful of her students getting "excited" about writing, displaying that joy, making their writing mobile through reciting and sharing it with their peers and desiring that the "I am from" model become a school-wide phenomenon? Didn't the students at this school, which primarily served working-class African American and Latinx children, deserve an opportunity to showcase their ways of knowing and being while expressing joy in writing?

One possible answer can be found in Prendergast's (2002) essential study of what she refers to as the "economy of literacy," where she examines how education and literacy became synonymous with Whiteness after the 1954 *Brown v. Board of Education* ruling that desegregated schools. Black and Brown students were expected to assimilate into American public schools rather than bring their full selves into the classroom.

Another answer comes from McHenry and Heath (1994), who argue that with the introduction of multicultural education, some teachers embraced "logos" for particular communities of learners. For example, Black children were construed as emerging from an oral tradition devoid of the written word. These logos ("Black children learn like A and Latinx children learn like B, while White children learn like C") were convenient yet oversimplified ways of thinking about students, their families, and cultures.

Diving more deeply, then, into the connections of language, literacy, race, and power, teachers should move beyond knowing that in the context of the United States it was illegal for enslaved Africans to learn to read, write, and, in many ways, think. Teachers should also learn about the ways in which people of African descent excavated pathways to access literacy and literacies. As the NCTE literacy brief asserts, merely implementing multicultural education is not enough to "foster cultural inclusiveness" (p. xvii; all page references to the literacy brief map to the version reprinted in the front matter of this book).

As teachers, all of us have experienced teaching and learning moments when we thought that simply introducing a book or material that celebrated diversity was the answer. But as we have learned, simple inclusion is not enough. In *Writing Instruction in the Culturally Relevant Classroom*, Maisha shared her story of using Richard Wright's *Black Boy* in an English class that primarily served African American students, only to learn from students that they were tired of reading books with Black characters who primarily experience poverty and other forms of despair (Winn & Johnson, 2011). To avoid that kind of response, we as teachers have to grow our body of knowledge around diversity and challenge ourselves to know more and do more. We have many resources to help us do this (some of which we introduce in this book), but we should also call on students and their families as valuable resources. As teachers, we cannot (nor should we pretend to) know everything. When we value multicultural perspectives in our classrooms, we can begin to do some of this important work. And we can learn from the work of others: the textual resources in this and other chapters are starting points to deepen our knowledge.

Resource Spotlight

McHenry, E., & Heath, S. B. (1994). "The Literate and the Literary: African Americans as Writers and Readers—1830–1940." *Written Communication, 11*(4), 419–44.

Why teachers should read this work:

- McHenry and Heath demonstrate how multicultural education invoked the use of "cultural logos," which prescribed teaching strategies for children in different ethnic groups.

- The authors argue that because African Americans are often celebrated as being "oral," their rich traditions in writing are often ignored.

Fisher, M. T. (2004). "'The Song Is Unfinished': The New Literate and Literary and Their Institutions." *Written Communication, 21*(3), 290–312.

Why teachers should read this work:

- Fisher extends McHenry and Heath's notion of the "literate and literary" through the Black Arts Movement and the resurgence of spoken word poetry open mics and writing workshops.

- Fisher demonstrates how people of African descent blur the boundaries between orality and literacy.

Prendergast, C. (2002). "The Economy of Literacy: How the Supreme Court Stalled the Civil Rights Movement." *Harvard Educational Review, 72*(2), 206–29.

Why teachers should read this work:

- Prendergast offers a compelling framework for how *Brown v. Board of Education* "racialized notions of literacy" (n.p.). This article is useful for ELA teachers because it traces how literacy became a form of "white property," thus making literacy and Whiteness synonymous.

A Restorative Justice in English Education Approach

What is this work that English teachers engage in when they demonstrably value multicultural perspectives and challenge themselves to continuously grow their knowledge? Throughout this book, we reference *restorative justice*—RJ—and other terms that are part of its constellation. While we provide a fuller definition of RJ in the next chapter, it is important to note here the journey that Maisha took toward understanding the intersectionality of the restorative justice paradigm and the field of English education. Early on in this work, Maisha imagined that writing and literacy teachers could engage students using a restorative paradigm that focused on selecting writing and reading experiences that build community and stimulate dialogue about race, class, gender, and identities. Using some of the process and approaches of RJ (to which you will be introduced in subsequent chapters), Maisha imagined restorative English education as a space for reading together and sharing ideas, explicating literature, brainstorming before writing, and sharing and exchanging writing. Over time, however, Maisha challenged her own omission of the word *justice* from *restorative English education*. Omitting *justice*, she began to see, ignores the legacy of inequity for many of our students. And because English language arts and writing teachers wield both power and promise in cultivating and sustaining inquisitive learning communities, we now see English teaching as an act of seeking justice for all children (Winn, 2016; Winn, 2018). Including the word *justice* is something we see as vital for cultivating and sustaining inquisitive learning communities where students *and* their teachers can engage in the critical conversations we must have in order to learn from and with each other. Throughout the book, then, we refer to a restorative justice English education to designate RJ possibilities specifically in the content area of English.

Engaging in Literacy for Purpose and Belonging

We turn now to *Adolescent Literacy: An NCTE Policy Research Brief*, seeking connections between this document and the background knowledge underlying restorative justice that we've raised thus far. All four dimensions of the brief connect in important ways that we further address in Chapter 3: (1) shifting literacy demands; (2) multiple and social literacies; (3) the importance of motivation; and (4) the value of multicultural perspectives.

To be sure, the brief's section on **shifting literacy demands** tells us that "[w]hen students are not recognized for bringing valuable, multiple-literacy practices to school, they can become resistant to school-based literacy" (p. xv). A restorative justice English education seeks to disrupt this cycle of devaluing because we know that this issue is often at the core of miscommunication, tensions, and challenges in relationships between students and teachers. When students are encouraged to write toward the goal of having purpose and cultivating belonging, they are able to write about issues that matter to them, including the lives of their families and their communities. To this end, adolescents should be able to "regularly use literacies for social and political purposes as they create meanings and participate in shaping their immediate environments" (p. xv). We want this for all our youth, for them to be able to communicate their valuable ideas through the act of writing, which has the power to organize and galvanize others into action.

Another dimension of adolescent literacy is the importance of acknowledging **multiple and social literacies**. According to the NCTE literacy brief, "Adolescent literacy is social, drawing from various discourse communities" (p. xv).

Similarly, our work introducing restorative justice in the English classroom is committed to valuing the historicized lives of both students and teachers and making these literacies *visible* in classroom communities. This dimension is a reminder to all of us who work with children and youth to access their funds of knowledge and funds of identity (Esteban-Guitart & Moll, 2014). Making students' literacies visible, acknowledging the new "literate and literary" (Fisher, 2004) and the types of writing our young people are engaged in, is critical. Maisha, for example, recently served as a judge for the Sacramento Area Youth Speaks (SAYS) Slam Finals. One of the poets explained to Maisha how she started hearing music in her mind and writing songs as early as elementary school. These songs launched her interest in other forms of writing. Many of the youth poets found membership and belonging in out-of-school writing communities like SAYS. Maisha also observed student artists engaged in playwriting in Regional Youth Detention Centers (RYDCs). Student artists reported to Maisha that writing and being a writer helped others see them as individuals beyond monolithic labels such as "delinquent," "at-risk," and "troubled" (Winn, 2011). Perhaps most important, because their teachers valued their writing and ideas and did not ask them to conform to any particular script in their playwriting, these students felt like citizens of this community of artists.

We cannot say enough about the **importance of motivation**. This book is committed to cultivating "responsive classroom environments," as outlined in the NCTE *Adolescent Literacy* brief (p. xvi). We know that creating a responsive teaching and learning environment is never in lieu of a rigorous academic experience; rather, the rigor will come because everyone knows and understands why they are there, how they are valued, and what the goals of the community are. We don't wish to exchange the "how" to write and read for the "why" we should be writing and reading. Once teachers create a responsive classroom environment that includes student choice and is centered on learners, we decrease the chance of confrontations, of students being ejected from or marginalized in classrooms, and thus ushered through a series of obsolete practices that lead to less instruction and learning time. We also question how teachers can begin to inspire motivation if there is a culture of isolating particular children by regularly sending them out of the classroom or positioning their opinions, viewpoints, and backgrounds as contradictory to teaching and learning goals. All students should feel they are citizens of the classroom—that is, that they are valued and thus feel invested in the community.

Thinking about how literacy is inextricably linked to notions of citizenship and belonging in the context of the United States (Ladson-Billings, 2005) is a way of deepening historical knowledge and understanding the moral imperative for all children to have access to reading, writing, language(s), and a way to engage the fourth dimension of adolescent literacy—**valuing multicultural perspectives**.

Resource Spotlight

Winn, M. T. (2013). "Forum: Toward a Restorative English Education." *Research in the Teaching of English, 48*(1), 126–35.

Why teachers should read this work:

- Winn offers a framework for teaching English that sits at the crossroads of restorative justice and education, or what she calls a "restorative teacher education."

- Winn argues that a restorative English education is "a pedagogy of possibilities that employs literature and writing to seek justice and restore (and, in some cases, create) peace that reaches beyond the classroom walls" (p. 127).

What we love most about this fourth and essential dimension is that NCTE urges teachers to move beyond being a "tourist" in other people's cultures to "critically confront and bridge social, cultural, and personal differences" (p. xvii). We believe the only way to truly engage in this is to engage in history. While English teachers may not be aware of the troubled relationship between literacy and people of color discussed earlier, they often embody this relationship in their practices because these ideas have been solidified and unthinkingly accepted over time. For example, values and practices in models of Western education sort learners based on ability. We should be alarmed that schools in the United States are experiencing more segregation now than at any time since the 1954 *Brown v. Board of Education* ruling. The persistence of segregation post-*Brown* should be on the forefront of all our minds (Noguera, Pierce, & Ahram, 2016). Davis (2012) reminds us that "histories never leave us for another inaccessible place. They are a part of us; they inhabit us and we inhabit them even when we are not aware of this relationship to history" (p. 185). The restorative justice work we are doing provides the opportunity to engage with history so that we can prepare young writers not just for their futures but also for their nows. This history enjoins us as educators to confront the discriminatory practices that have haunted the profession and the young people we teach every day so that we might begin the process of restoration. Learning our histories and their manifestation in our current state of education is the beginning of that process. It is our hope that the texts mentioned and cited in this chapter will aid you in commencing or continuing your own journey toward a more just and equitable classroom.

Restorative Justice in Educative Spaces

I n the prologue and Chapter 1, we began to introduce you to restorative justice principles and their necessity in the English language arts classroom—a restorative justice English education. In this chapter, we step back to ground this work more generally in some of its historical roots, particularly in a restorative justice in education methodology, an approach that impacts entire scholastic systems, including English classrooms.

The practices of restorative justice in education (RJE) have their roots in Indigenous cultural wisdom and were introduced to the Western justice system in the early 1980s and applied in schools in the early 1990s by educators and RJE advocates. A genuine appreciation and understanding of the inherent wisdom embodied in these practices guides both ELA teachers and teachers more generally in applying these strategies sensitively and creatively to our present-day classroom contexts. While we see this book as an introduction to these practices, we suggest that those interested in learning and implementing RJE in their own classrooms participate in training facilitated by experienced RJE trainers, who can delve more deeply into these practices and help participants avoid common pitfalls, including those that might be counterproductive for their class-rooms. Such training can remind educators of what they already know and do that reflects restorative principles. In this training, teachers learn how to bring a restorative justice education to youth in classrooms, experiencing and applying RJE processes in a practical yet authentic way through role-play and other experiential exercises. Most training includes self-reflection, sharing lived experiences, and telling our own stories. Reflecting on our own stories and heritage and remembering how our ancestors may have participated in restorative practices can connect teachers authentically to the practices of present-day restorative justice.

Cole Middle School

We begin with Oakland Unified School District's (OUSD) Cole Middle School as an example of a successful school-wide introduction and implementation of RJE, from 2006 to 2009. Rita was fortunate to have an inside view of this process as she was on staff at Cole and integral to the introduction of RJE to the school. Sumner and colleagues (2010) documented that when Cole staff used RJE in classrooms and in the school more generally, over the course of three years Cole reduced suspensions by 87 percent (p. 3), with only one mandatory exclusion. Sumner et al. also noted that the school increased effective student participation, accountability, and leadership. On top of all this, Cole retained 100 percent of its teachers. The staff was proud that they didn't lose either adults or young people, nor their gifts and talents. Sadly, many present structures in education and the juvenile justice system experience loss of youth when they tend to criminalize and marginalize poor youth, youth with special needs, and youth of color in our schools. But Cole was able to avoid this tendency.

How did Cole staff achieve these successes? To introduce RJE, Rita and her colleagues began with the adults. As a school staff, they reflected critically on their teaching, learning, and disciplinary practices, wondering if the school was unintentionally aiding in a process of great human loss by participating in the school-to-prison pipeline. Through their reflection, they noticed that many young people and their families experienced layer upon layer of trauma. They witnessed families becoming vulnerable to economic challenges, especially when the 2008 recession hit, losing their homes and having to move away from family and friends to new neighborhoods. They saw their young people become more vulnerable to drug use, violence, juvenile detention, suicide, homicide, and early death. Rita and the school staff found themselves suffering vicarious trauma. Committed to finding ways to work with their students and families, they asked themselves: *How can we reverse the trend of losing our own well-being and that of our youth, and begin the process of healing for all at Cole?* In this chapter, we build on the lessons of Cole as we explore how restorative justice can be used as a school-wide and classroom-specific tool to, first, acknowledge and address ways to build relationships that create a strong class and school community, and second, reduce harm that occurs in our teaching and learning spaces. The questions we address are these:

- How can stakeholders within a school build strong relationships and communities that are welcoming and engender a sense of belonging for all adults and all students?

- What are the tools associated with restorative justice in education that can be used by stakeholders to reduce harm, address harm when it occurs, and promote healing?

- How can we, the school community, welcome adults and students who, in the process of reentry, have made amends to people they have harmed so that they will be fully accepted into our school and classroom communities?

At Cole, Rita and the school staff had to think about what was going on in schools on both micro and macro levels. They had to grapple with the evidence that schools using punitive disciplinary practices were pushing youth out of schools so that they oftentimes landed in the streets with no guidance. The following section reviews some of the macro circumstances that are particularly relevant to RJE practitioners in schools.

Losing Our Children: How Schools Are Implicated

Zero Tolerance and Suspensions

Recent alarming reports have emerged about negative school experiences of even very young children. In an NPR report, Cory Turner (2016) noted that the US Department of Education acknowledged that 6,743 children enrolled in the pre-kindergarten classes provided by the public school system were suspended at least once or more in the 2013–14 school year. This doesn't include the additional number of children suspended from private preschools. School sites and districts all over the nation are accustomed to using punitive measures as a rule rather than the exception. This practice is a continuation of schools enforcing zero tolerance policies, which research shows harms schools and communities rather than creating more order and safety (American Psychological Association, 2008).

Fabelo et al. (2011) found that 59.6 percent of students experienced at least one suspension or expulsion in secondary public schools. Their study shows that in the majority of cases the administrator could have used other strategies to deal with the situation, noting that "only 3 percent of students had broken rules that made suspension or expulsion a required punishment, such as carrying a weapon to school" (p. 10). Reports on the more serious incidents include specific criteria, whereas the less serious incidents are more dependent on the lens and discretion of the person in a position to exclude the youth from the learning environment (Losen & Orfield, 2002; Morgan, Salomon, Plotkin, & Cohen, 2014; Staats, 2014). Fabelo and colleagues also point out that Black students and students with disabilities were more likely to be suspended or expelled.

Fabelo et al. (2011) also stated that students who were suspended were twice as likely to drop out of school or be held back a grade. They further noted that students who are suspended and expelled from school are, in turn, significantly more likely to become caught up in the juvenile justice system. This routing or funneling of students from schools directly into the justice system has come to be known as the "school to prison pipeline" (p. 7).

Poverty and Adverse Childhood Experiences Study (ACES)

Many of the students being suspended in schools are children living in poverty. The Children's Defense Fund reports that in 2015 there were more than 14.5 million children experiencing poverty and many of them were children of color (p. 1). Children experiencing poverty enter schools with unmet needs-related traumas connected to conditions of poor health, inadequate access to appropriate health care, and life circumstances that hinder optimal social, emotional, and neurological development.

In fact, a Centers for Disease Control-Kaiser Permanente study found that traumas early in life or "adverse childhood experiences (ACEs)" can cause damage to the developing brain and increase risk for mental, physical, and emotional illness later in life. The ACEs study found that a high number of adverse childhood experiences is "at the root of most violence" (ACES Too High, n.d.).

Zero tolerance and strict suspension/expulsion policies have not paid attention to an individual's human developmental processes or to the root causes of other serious life challenges. While zero tolerance might make sense in cases of serious, violent violations, these policies have too often been used to justify harsh actions when a youth is acting as young people do: talking out loud, having a conflict with a peer or teacher, or being unable to control emotions (without doing any violence) in class.

Why Punishment Doesn't Work

As the statistics recounted in the previous section highlight, school cultures are far too often mired in a punishment-oriented approach to children. Punishment is the go-to strategy used in the justice system, detention facilities, many schools, and some homes and communities. Punishing youth "for their own good" has been a common practice in most cultures throughout US history. But punishment doesn't serve the well-being of our young people, educators, schools, or communities in an equitable and just society. Harming people to show that harming others is wrong is counterproductive and not conducive to community building and healing harm, nor does it make our communities safer.

It is important to remember that we have set up a society in which young people do not have formal power, money, or status and are thus susceptible to disrespect, disempowerment, and distrust by the adults around them. They suffer even more if they are from disenfranchised communities. Young people have always challenged adults by testing cultural limits and mores. Adults then have the choice of either listening deeply, working to understand and learn from young people who are literally society's future, or trying to control them to fit into our societal molds.

We recognize that even in the face of such challenges and adversity, young people remain resilient. But as Amanda J. Moreno reminds us, "Resilience does not mean that children 'get over it.' It does mean that the caring adults in their lives have a lot of power to buffer, rather than cement, the effects of toxic stress" (qtd. in Prevent Child Abuse America & KPJR Films, 2016, p. 3). Many educators are front-line caring adults who can intervene to ensure children's well-being by exercising their power to notice, engage, respond to, and triage students' situations, and refer them to trauma professionals if necessary. Moving toward a more restorative, accountable, and just education can begin to meet the needs of *all* our children and possibly even bring a healing balm to the most vulnerable of youth and families. This approach can reduce the impact of adverse experiences and allow a young person even in the throes of trauma to be relieved of its effects in the classroom. This role in supporting resilience is one of the possibilities that comes with agreement among the adults in schools on using restorative—rather than punitive—approaches to education.

RJE does not imply or encourage permissiveness. Indeed, it is essential that classrooms develop strong communities with guidelines that spell out cooperative and collaborative behaviors and accountability practices that model ways to problem-solve and practice values such as respect, empathy, inclusion, and gratitude. As the teachers at Cole Middle School found, RJE practices help students, teachers, and others to identify with one another's humanity and individual identities, and to build strong, civic-acting

Figure 2.1. Artwork by Lilla Watson.

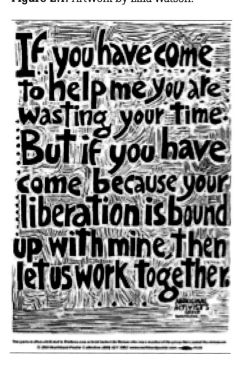

people. This book is dedicated to the purpose of finding the healthiest, heart- and mind-centered, wisest ways to respond to young people in our schools. *Together*, adults and young people in schools can liberate themselves by working toward the common goal of mutual respect. This goal is conveyed in Figure 2.1 (p. 15) through the artwork and quote by Lilla Watson, an Australian Indigenous artist and social justice activist.

Constructing the Container

At Cole Middle School, recognizing that schools can play a role in the negative experiences of youth, particularly minoritized youth, the staff wanted to be a part of the solution, changing school and classroom practices to eradicate force and fear in the school culture. As mentioned earlier, the first step was to adopt RJE practices with adults in the school. In the first year of implementation, Cole set aside four full days for an RJE training and one staff meeting per month for all the adults to connect in an RJE Circle practice. Circles (as we discuss more fully later in this chapter) are a common RJE activity in which people gather, sit in a circle, and have conversations in a structured way, using a talking piece (i.e., an object that is meaningful to the group) so that every voice is heard. In adult-only circles at Cole, staff learned about one another and even worked out disagreements. Surprisingly—with a focus on just the adults, no students involved—Cole's statistics at the end of the first year showed a 20 percent decrease in fights between students and a 20 percent decrease in suspensions. Staff members were more connected and their relationships had deepened through the RJE practices. The staff at Cole made a commitment to be less punitive and to use these restorative practices with all of their students.

The Seven Core Assumptions

What were the assumptions that guided the work at Cole? Rita and the staff understood that particular beliefs and values would guide them as they began their journey, because to be restorative is a mindset and heart change. Boyes-Watson and Pranis (2015) entreat us to begin by engaging with the "Seven Core Assumptions" about human beings (pp. 9–17). (See Figure 2.2, a poster by Living Justice Press listing the assumptions.) At Cole, the staff committed to changing their relationships with each other and with their students and families. For this to happen, they needed to become more conscious of how they used their personal and professional power.

Figure 2.2. The restorative justice seven core assumptions about human beings. (This and other similar posters reproduced in this book are used with permission by and are available from Living Justice Press. This publisher offers these documents free of charge to anyone for personal, educational, or training purposes. They are print quality and can be used as posters [they can be enlarged up to 300 percent for posters], handouts, overheads, or parts of a Circle centerpiece. These documents are copyrighted by Living Justice Press, which asks that the documents not be posted or used online without proper attribution, along with a link to their website at www.livingjusticepress.org. For questions on re-use or permissions, please contact ljpress@aol.com or call 651-695-1008.)

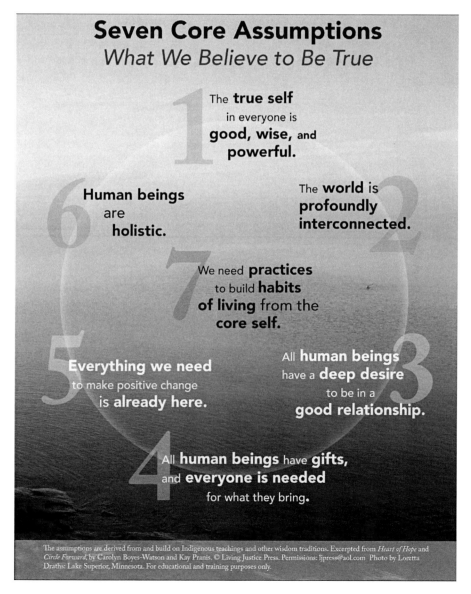

The Relationship Matrix: Use of Power in Schools, Adult-Youth Relating

The relationship matrix diagram in Figure 2.3 by Evans and Vaandering (2016) presents different ways to think about how we treat one another and ultimately our students. It highlights how high expectations and a high level of support honor and allow the sharing of power, while anything less than that treats people as objects who need to be managed or ignored.

Figure 2.3. The relationship matrix. (Reprinted from *Restorative Justice in Education* by Katherine Evans and Dorothy Vaandering by permission of Good Books, an imprint of Skyhorse Publishing. Inc.)

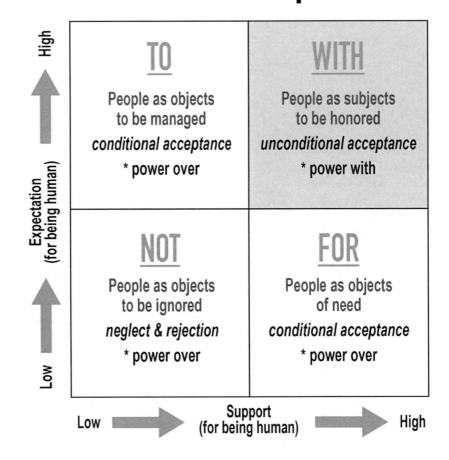

The Relationship Matrix

TO
People as objects
to be managed
conditional acceptance
* power over

WITH
People as subjects
to be honored
unconditional acceptance
* power with

NOT
People as objects
to be ignored
neglect & rejection
* power over

FOR
People as objects
of need
conditional acceptance
* power over

Expectation (for being human): Low → High

Support (for being human): Low → High

From Restorative Justice in Education by Katherine Evans and Dorothy Vaandering / Good Books, New York

The staff at Cole came to understand that the ideal way to honor a person is to accept the person unconditionally and to share power "with" the person rather than have power "over" them. "Doing with" honors each person as a human being deserving of dignity and respect. "Doing with" puts aside our implicit or explicit biases and leads us to work together with the individual, be they a colleague, a preschooler, or a high schooler. In contrast, "doing to" or "doing for" discourages individual agency and, in many instances, negates the power of the individual to feel, think, or act. At a 2017 conference in Minnesota, RJE practitioner and trainer Mary Skillings taught that most of us move between these two quadrants, the "to" and the "for," until we're exhausted, which is when we may cope by ignoring or neglecting people and their needs. The quadrant that RJE encourages us to locate ourselves in is the top right quadrant in Figure 2.3, the "with" quadrant, where we are very conscious of what each individual is thinking, doing, and feeling. And with such conscious presence and attunement to the "other" person, we can make decisions together for the good of all the people most affected by the decisions to be made.

These relationship matrixes can be applied to groups as well.

Most of us operate from all four quadrants. The challenge is to remember that we may be responding in a way that isn't helpful for our students or colleagues, and if so, to catch ourselves and then change our responses to be more restorative. Self-care plays a very important role here. Without self-care, we may not have the energy or spaciousness within ourselves to be restorative with others. Self-care is a necessity in RJE work.

The teachers at Cole understood the big picture of what was happening with their school. They had begun relationship building with one another and were anxious to understand more about restorative justice in education. They asked themselves: What is restorative justice, what is restorative justice in education, and how do we implement RJE with our students?

What Is Restorative Justice?

So, what is restorative justice, and how can it help frame what we could be doing better in schools? Both restorative and retributive or punitive approaches to justice have coexisted throughout time. Restorative justice philosophy, principles, and practices have roots in ancient and Indigenous ways and wisdom from all over the world: South Africa's Truth and Reconciliation Commission (TRC); the Rwandan Gacaca Courts (Hauschildt, 2012); the New Zealand Maori, whose community leaders and parents pushed the juvenile justice system to learn about and introduce restorative justice using the practice of family group conferences (MacRae & Zehr, 2004); the First Peoples in Australia, who founded Koori, Nunga, and Murri

Courts (Marchetti & Daly, 2004); the Americas, with Indigenous responses to harm doing and community healing in Mexico and Central and South America (J. Tello, 2017); and North American practices of First Nations in Canada and First Peoples in the United States. We can even trace the roots of restorative justice to ancient civilizations, including Arab, Greek, Roman, Indian Vedic, Buddhist, and Taoist traditions (Braithwaite, 2002, p. 3). Reflecting on our own heritage and studying how our ancestors participated in restorative practices can be helpful in grounding teachers in the philosophy of restorative justice and connecting them to present-day efforts and practices.

Restorative justice was initiated into the Western justice system in the early 1980s and subsequently introduced into schools in the early 1990s by educators and advocates. In response to an assault at a school event in a Queensland, Australia, high school in 1994, Marg Thorsborne, an Australian educator, drew on a model of the restorative conference (O'Connell, 1998). Following the successful resolution of this incident, various government bodies provided funding for restorative justice education to be implemented in 100 Queensland schools (Cameron & Thorsborne, 2001). Since then, RJE has been widely adopted in Australia and New Zealand and has spread to the United Kingdom, other European countries, and the United States and Canada. RJE is growing exponentially, and the results are promising, showing improved relationships in the classroom, school, district, and community; a reduction in suspensions and expulsions; and improved test scores (Fronius, Persson, Guckenburg, Hurley, & Petrosino, 2016, p. 27).

According to Brenda Morrison (2005), restorative justice is a philosophy, a set of principles, and a set of practices that attend to connectedness through *affirming*, *repairing*, and *rebuilding* relationships. Lorraine Stutzman Amstutz and Judy Mullet emphasize that RJE is an effort to build relationships and community based on values, paying attention to needs, and healing (2005):

> Restorative Justice promotes values and principles that use inclusive, collaborative approaches for being in community. These approaches validate the experiences and needs of everyone within the community, particularly those who have been marginalized, oppressed or harmed. These approaches allow us to act and respond in ways that are healing rather than alienating or coercive. (p. 15)

Complementing this sentiment, Morrison (2012) states that RJE is a socially and emotionally intelligent justice that embraces social engagement instead of social control. In other words, everyone in schools—from adults to youth—needs to acknowledge and understand their own emotions, as well as nurture the ability to empathize with others about their emotions, all of which has a positive impact on relationships. When emotionally intelligent adults attune themselves to what young people need, they can craft an effective learning environment in which students can be successful; likewise, when students grow in emotional intelligence, they can discern both what they need and how to ask for what they need rather than merely reacting or acting out in class.

Elaborating even further on RJE, Jon Kidde and Rita Alfred (2011) explain:

> Restorative Justice is a philosophy and an approach to discipline that moves away from punishment toward restoring a sense of harmony and well-being for all those affected by a hurtful act. It provides families, schools, and communities a way to ensure accountability while at the same time breaking the cycle of retribution and violence. It is based on a view of resilience in children and youth and their capability to solve problems, as opposed to the youth themselves being the problems adults must fix. It focuses not on retribution but on reconnecting severed relationships and re-empowering individuals by holding them responsible. This approach acknowledges that, when a person does harm, it affects the persons they hurt, the community, and themselves. When using restorative measures, an attempt is made to repair the harm caused by one person to another and to the community so that everyone is moved toward healing. (p. 9)

RJE can thus be seen as a preventative measure because it focuses on building a strong community that engenders belonging, intervention when harm is caused, and reintegration into the school community after exclusion from class or school occurs. RJE has been shown to be effective in situations requiring some disciplinary process. We use the word *discipline* intentionally here, because while in our culture *discipline* has become synonymous with punishment, its Latin origins suggest something different. In Latin, *disciplina* means "instruction," and its root, *discere*, means "to learn." To discipline, then, is to instruct and teach versus to punish. RJE does exactly that—it provides a strong community foundation upon which students can reflect on their actions when they cause harm, learn from the experience, and figure out what needs to be done to heal the harm.

These definitions of restorative justice education demonstrate an evolution in both the definition and the use of restorative justice in schools that is different from restorative justice in the court and justice systems. Implementing RJE tasks us to think about what it means to educate *human beings*, and how we educate within a *community* of teachers and learners in a school. Schools like Cole that are implementing RJE have moved away from punishing to specifically teaching about behaviors that enhance learning, and they are addressing behavior as individual and separate from what is happening in the community or class. This attitude holds that RJE is not merely a set of practices (though practices are involved), but rather an *approach* to considering the well-being of all people in educative spaces. Evans and Vaandering (2016) build on this concept by asking us to acknowledge and hold the preciousness and worth of every human being as central to RJE. They push us to consider moving away from the American ideal of individualism to realize that both individual and collective well-being can be better supported through notions of cooperation than through competition, defining RJE as "facilitating learning communities that nurture the capacity of people to engage with one another and their environment in a manner that supports and respects the inherent dignity and worth of all" (p. 11).

Restorative Justice in Schools and Classrooms: A Three-Tiered Approach

A distinction of RJE practices in schools as compared to those in the justice system is that in schools a community-building component is essential to beginning and sustaining an ongoing environment of respect, dignity, mutual concern, growth, and learning. The process of building community involves laying a foundation in individual classrooms and throughout the school to ensure that every member of that community is respected and heard. In this community-building approach, each member—from student, to teacher, to administrator, to staff, to parents—is supported in ways that make clear this work is each person's responsibility.

For all stakeholders in the school community to achieve social engagement rather than social control in the classroom, Brenda Morrison proposed that schools follow a three-tiered approach of relational interactions (2007). Morrison's pyramidal diagram illustrating this three-tiered approach (p. 116) was further revised by Kidde and Alfred in 2014 (see Figure 2.4. for the previously unpublished version).

Tier 1 consists of the daily interactional practices that build relationships to strengthen class and school communities. We find that when all adults and youth participate in tier 1 activities, more of both are ready to actively engage with each other, teaching and learning in a good way. Tier 2 consists of structured practices that make space for conflicts and misunderstandings.[8] Tier 3 practices are designed to help in the more intense conflict situations, including reentry and reintegration after exclusion from class or school. In the next sections, we explain each tier, highlight some of the practices underlying each one, and suggest how schools might put these practices into effect.

Tier 1: Building and Strengthening Relationships

Most of the RJE work in classrooms centers on tier 1 activities. The base of the model, Tier 1: Build and Strengthen Relationships, contains the fundamental relational practices of caring and developing values and norms for all members of the school community: students, adults, families, and even active community members. Central to this tier are "Circles," which, according to Indigenous practices, Carolyn Boyes-Watson and Pranis (2015) explain, build connection in the

Figure 2.4. A whole-school model of restorative justice in education. (Reprinted with permission from *Restoring Safe School Communities* by Brenda Morrison, The Federation Press, Sydney, Australia, 2007.)

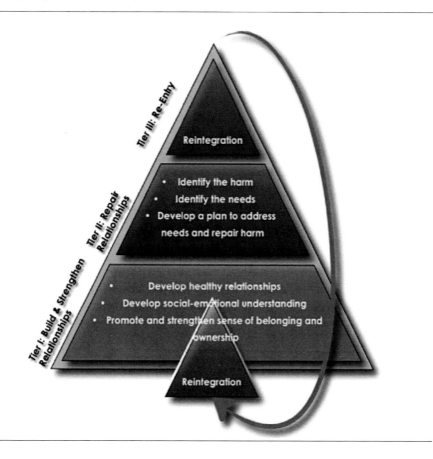

school and classroom (p. 399). The Circle process (adapted from the Peacemaking Circles taught to early RJ pioneers in the 1980s by the Tagish-Tlingit First Nations people of the Yukon, Canada) is a way of holding intentional conversations. Fundamental to the process of restorative justice, Circles encourage all members of a community to gather, physically see one another, engage in community-building practices, and share stories. In this chapter, we focus on Circle practices as a means to create, nurture, and repair relationships. However, Circles are not the sole means to creating a restorative environment (as we discuss in more depth in Chapters 3, 4, and 5). Bringing a restorative mindset to community building, where students are authentically invited to join and contribute to communities, is an essential component of RJE.

In Figure 2.5, the Balancing Relationship-Building and Problem-Solving poster, depicts the four relational elements of the Circle practice taught by Indigenous leaders and adopted by RJE practitioners—a balance of relationship building and problem solving as participants get acquainted, building understanding and

Figure 2.5. Poster depicting the elements in balancing relationship building and problem solving.

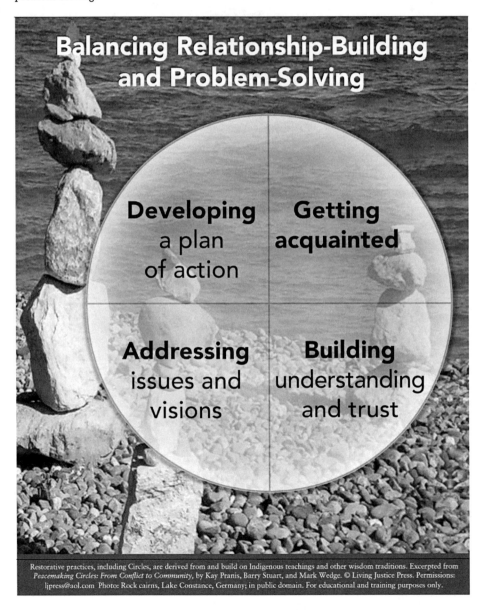

trust, discussing issues and concerns, and, when necessary and needed, making agreements or a plan. We have found that for any project to be completed in a restorative manner, at least 50 percent of the time allotted is devoted to getting acquainted and building trust. When project teams follow that restorative way, they are most often successful and much happier when they complete their project.

Community-Building Circles

To introduce RJE in the classroom, we suggest class communities begin with Circles focused on community building: getting to know one another and building trust. As the trust builds, you can move from getting-to-know-you and trust-building Circles to Circles focused more on issues and concerns (and, as we explain in Chapter 5, on curriculum).

Community-Building Circle practices encourage creativity, a grounding in values, adherence to behavioral agreements, implementation of democratic processes through consensus decision making, sharing of multifaceted stories, discussion of issues, making action agreements, and conducting follow-up on any issues or concerns. These Circles develop team building through self-challenging and self-reflective exercises that allow members to develop relationships, share about themselves, and learn about one another and themselves in ways that allow everyone to feel that they belong in the classroom.

There are many different kinds of Community-Building Circles. You can build community through Circles that celebrate successes and joys and have fun; through academic support Circles, as when supporting students before they take tests; through healing Circles, when the students and adults in class or school experience grief and need support to process loss, perhaps due to devastating school or local shootings. These Circles move a class and school from an "I" frame to a "We" frame, as in the South African concept of "Ubuntu," which translates as "I am because We are."

Elements of a Community-Building Circle. The elements of a Community-Building Circle include the following:

- Seating all the participants in a circle with an open space in the middle.
- Conducting an opening and a closing, the ceremonial parts of the Circle process. Ceremonies are special rituals that act as a container to "hold" what goes on in the space.
- Introducing a centerpiece to hold all the work (values, guidelines, artistic expressions) that will be done in the Circle.
- Following particular structures, such as
   ○ Using a talking piece,

- ○ Determining and agreeing on values, and
- ○ Creating and agreeing on guidelines.
- Asking guiding questions for the discussion.
- Implementing an agreement if needed (for instance, when making decisions after the discussion).
- Concluding with a reflection of how this Circle affected each person.
- Ending with a closing.

In addition, it's important to note that Circles are led by a trained Circle Keeper.

Seating. Circle participants physically gather together to engage in community-building practices (see Figure 2.6). To set up the physical space, if possible, arrange chairs in a circle without any furniture in the middle or between participants.

Figure 2.6. Various seating arrangements for Circles.

This may not be possible in some classrooms. We have tried numerous configurations: We have pushed all tables to the middle and sat around the tables. We've made a circle with our tables and sat on the tables. We have broken the class into two groups and one group met elsewhere in the school. We have stood against the walls in the science lab.

Whatever way works for your space, remember that your configuration must be conducive to both light and deep conversations.

Openings and Closings. Circles begin and end by bringing the group together to sign off as a community. Songs, movement, meditation, mindfulness moments, cooperative and fun games, and team-building exercises are just a few possible openings and closings. Some schools are extra sensitive about incorporating symbols that suggest religious beliefs, so knowing and educating your community is important when you are choosing activities.

The Centerpiece. The center or focal point of a Circle is often represented by a piece of beautiful fabric placed in the middle of the space. Most centers invoke nature through symbols of fire, water, air, and earth. Because many schools and other buildings don't allow the use of candles, some Circle practitioners use the electric candles that can be turned on and off. The center reflects the discussions, thoughts, feelings, and other expressions of the Circle participants and grows as participants are invited to place items there. Such items might include special or symbolic objects that belong to participants; values captured on construction paper, paper plates, or hand cutouts like the ones in Figure 2.7; a list of core guidelines. Other meaningful objects that could be used as talking pieces may also sit at the center.

Figure 2.7. Examples of Circle centerpieces.

Following Particular Structures: Talking Pieces. The use of talking pieces may be familiar to many teachers as something that is passed around a circle to indicate whose turn it is to speak. Every pass around the circle is considered a round. The talking piece helps to structure participant interactions by ensuring that only one person speaks at a time, that everyone has an opportunity to speak, and that everyone takes responsibility for listening when not holding the talking piece.

Talking pieces are most effective when they are special objects that are meaningful and appropriate to the group. In many Native American traditions, the talking piece is first passed to the left, following the direction of our hearts. It is then passed in that same direction as it moves around the Circle from person to person. It is not passed across the Circle, nor in a reversed direction. In RJ Circles, everyone waits to receive the talking piece as it comes around. The discipline of waiting to use the talking piece teaches lessons in patience and humility as we wait for our turn to speak (see Figure 2.8).

Following Particular Structures: Determining and Agreeing on Values and Guidelines. A Circle process continues with the group coming to some consensus about the values and guidelines that participants can agree on. Values are the foundation for their engagement and help everyone understand

Figure 2.8. Examples of talking pieces.

that this is a special conversation and everyone is invited to bring their best selves. Values can be written on cardstock or paper plates and placed in the middle of the Circle space. See the common Circle values in Figure 2.9. We recommend that for purposes of strong classroom ownership and belonging, each class should develop and agree on their own classroom values.

Figure 2.9. A poster outlining a set of common Circle values.

Common Circle Values

Love

Honesty

Respect

Humility

Members of each Circle explore together the values they want to bring to the process. These are some examples.

Inclusivity

Empathy

Generosity

Sharing

Trust

Courage

Restorative practices, including Circles, are derived from and build on Indigenous teachings and other wisdom traditions. Excerpted from *Peacemaking Circles: From Conflict to Community*, by Kay Pranis, Barry Stuart, and Mark Wedge. © Living Justice Press. Permissions: ljpress@aol.com Photo by Loretta Draths: Baptism River, Minnesota. For educational and training purposes only.

Guidelines help to indicate the participant behaviors that are necessary to create the best conditions in the Circle so that each person can bring his or her best self to the group. Figure 2.10 shows the common Circle guidelines that many people in RJE Circles use (adapted from Boyes-Watson and Pranis's *Circle Forward*

Figure 2.10. A poster outlining a set of common Circle guidelines.

[2015]). Similar to the process for developing and agreeing on Circle values, each class is encouraged to create, agree on, and practice their own Circle guidelines that they can use and revisit over the course of their Circle practices. Students can choose guidelines worded in their own cultural and language style that convey the following: use only one mic; offer sincere, honest communication; respect everyone; listen to everyone; be considerate of sharing the time; and keep conversations that happen in Circle private and confidential except for mandatory reporting issues. Some groups doing RJE include "Say just enough" as a reminder to long-winded talkers. (See below for more on how to initiate a values round.)

Implementing Discussions and Agreements. During discussion rounds, the group engages in building or strengthening their relationships with one another or, if needed, problem solving. They can do this by telling their lived stories to get to know each other and build trust. In an ELA class, participants can share their creative writing exercises or their class projects. They can also use the discussion round to talk about issues and concerns that are affecting them in the class or in school. These discussion rounds can, but do not have to, end with an agreement or plan that the class or school will complete. If the Circle ends with an agreement or plan, we advise that a follow-up Circle be implemented to review the progress of the agreement or plan. And when the agreement or plan is completed successfully, doing a follow-up Celebration Circle is recommended.

Concluding with Reflection. The reflection round helps Circle participants consider what they have learned, what may have surprised them, the connections they have made, and, more generally, how they have been affected by what they have heard and felt. The invitation in this round is to move toward the conclusion of the Circle, so we caution against asking a question or using a prompt that will encourage participants to reengage with the subject matter.

Guiding Questions for Community-Building Circles

A Circle can be used for a wide variety of reasons, and questions posed by the Circle Keeper focus the conversation.[9] The questions follow a path from getting-to-know-you subjects to questions and activities that build understanding and trust.[10] Some sample questions, from light to more personal, include:

1. Getting Acquainted
   - If you had a superpower, what would it be and how would you use it?
   - What is your favorite dish to eat? Describe how you would cook it.

2. Building Understanding and Trust

- If you could speak to anyone from the/your past, present, or future, who would that person be and what question would you ask him or her?
- What are some values you hold that you learned in childhood?
- What is an experience in your life when you made "lemonade out of lemons"?

3. Discussing Issues and Concerns

- Does class size matter?
- What should we do about students coming late to class?
- What is happening in this class/school that worries you?
- Should parents limit your time on your tech devices?
- What can we do about cyberbullying?
- If there was one thing that hasn't yet been said that could help us reach a deeper level of understanding/clarity, what would it be?

4. Making Agreements and Plans

- What? Who? When? How?
- Who will do _____?
- When will _____ be done by [date]?
- Who will monitor the plan?
- What will we do if the plan is not followed?
- What do we do to celebrate?

The Circle Keeper

Circles are led by a trained Circle Keeper, a role that requires you to be aware, conscious, open, compassionate, and empathetic. The Circle Keeper initiates the Circle by welcoming participants to the space and then following certain steps to invite participation (see Figure 2.11). For any portions of the Circle that require participation, the Circle Keeper passes the talking piece. As the group works through various rounds of discussion, agreement, and reflection, the talking piece repeatedly makes its way around the Circle.

When in a Circle, the Circle Keeper does not interrupt anyone who is talking but waits to receive the talking piece to talk. It's very important for the Circle Keeper to model this kind of discipline. However, the Circle Keeper may interrupt if he or she perceives that a harm is taking place or a harm is going to take place. Even seasoned Circle Keepers find it helpful to prepare a plan for the Circle ahead of time.

Figure 2.11. Circle guide sheet.

Sample questions to pose to your classroom community:	(Possible) methods for posing questions:
• What does our classroom community need? What do you need from our classroom community? • Are there any issues or concerns that need to be discussed? • How could a Circle assist our classroom community? • What do you want participants to walk away from our next Circle feeling or thinking about? • What should be the focus of our next Circle?	• Ask students to write responses on strips of paper; compile these and read them aloud, discussing as a class. • Ask students to write responses on sticky notes and group these categorically. Discuss these as a class. • Ask students to engage in a "chalk talk," in which each student stands with a marker in front of a large piece of butcher paper or whiteboard and writes responses, building on and adding to others' responses as they write. Discuss as a class.

Examples of Community-Building Circles from Circle Forward

1. Values Circle. We recommend starting Circle practice in your classroom with a Values Circle. The "Exploring Our Values-in-Action Circle," one of more than 100 ready-made Circles described in Boyes-Watson and Pranis's 2015 *Circle Forward* (p. 62), goes through the Circle process, first asking students to write on a paper plate a value that is important to them and that will communicate to others how they want to be treated. Students then share that value, followed by the teacher collecting all the paper plates and leading the reflection and closing rounds. The teacher may then, on another day, bring the collection of values that students generated to see if they can hold these values as a class. This may take some negotiating among the participants. Once the values are agreed upon, the class can make posters or artistic artifacts that they place in their classrooms to remind themselves about their agreed-upon values. When anyone in the classroom forgets to follow the values, the teacher can gently remind them, both at Circle time and during regular class time. The values become part of the way class members treat one another, the staff, and even their environment. In the ELA classroom, the discussion of values can be ongoing and students can be asked to notice the presence or absence of those values in the literature they are reading. They can also write about these values, make speeches about them, act them out, or write poetry like haiku.

Here's an example of how a Values Circle can work in the classroom. Stephanie worked with Rita at Cole Middle School as a teacher, and she now teaches and is an RJE practitioner in a Los Angeles middle school. In an RJE class she taught to middle schoolers in Daly City in 2014, she began by asking the class to rearrange their tables and chairs to form a circle.

To start thinking about the values they might want to adopt as a class, Stephanie had the students write a story about whether they had ever been harmed in any way in previous classrooms. She assured them that these stories were for them only and that they wouldn't have to share them with anyone, including her. After the writing exercise, she collected the stories and sealed them in a tin can. Stephanie and the students then talked about how they felt writing out their experiences. Understanding that this writing may have recalled some difficult emotions, after the reflection round and for the closing, Stephanie invited students to shake it off with a somatic exercise that ended the Circle.

The next day they returned to the Circle and used these painful stories to think together about the values they could hold as a class so they wouldn't have such experiences again. They wrote these values on a chart. For the next round, each person spoke about the values and whether any of them would be difficult to uphold. When they ended up with the final list, they made posters to remind themselves about the values they had agreed on. They posted these on the classroom walls.

Thereafter, when Stephanie was teaching and saw a student not following the class values, all she had to do was point either to the values chart or to the tin can that she guarded but kept displayed to remind the student to follow the agreed-upon values. She saved a lot of time not having to stop class to have a conversation with the student. It was also a restorative way to *remind* rather than *punish* students for not adhering to the values agreement (Kingdon, personal communication, 2014).

2. Relationship-Building Circles. Another useful Circle found in Boyes-Watson and Pranis's *Circle Forward* (2015) is the Relationship-Building Circle, a helpful one for classrooms because it focuses on building, deepening, understanding, repairing, and rebuilding relationships (p. 101). This Circle includes various rounds, beginning with a relaxing mindfulness exercise, followed by a second round of developing values and using the values to construct guidelines that will influence the behavior of Circle participants. Then Circle members move into introductions and check-in.

The purpose of this Relationship-Building Circle is for participants to get to know one another. In the discussion or activity round, they are asked to draw what they would like to share about themselves and then partner with someone to share the drawing. Three more rounds follow, with participants sharing something they value about their families, community, or neighborhood; something they learned about the others in Circle; and one word about how they are feeling. The Circle ends with a closing.

Classrooms that begin with a Relationship-Building Circle rarely send students out of class for disciplinary action, because they have built a sense of community. The rate of student attendance and engagement is high, and students' mindful presence in the classroom during instruction ensures that they don't fall behind in their learning.

When there is a strong beginning and ongoing, structured Circle space in the classroom, participants are able to express thoughts and feelings. Compassion and understanding cultivated in the Circle can contribute to healing since the trustworthiness developed through the Circle is the antidote to the wounds of trauma. The experience of belonging builds trust, and trust holds people together. (See Appendixes 3 and 4 for templates that can be used to plan out a Circle and a guide sheet explaining each step in the process.)

Guess Who's Coming to Circle

To begin the use of Circles with young people, we must be cognizant of who they are and the stage of their human development. Depending on students' ages, developmental stages, and other forms of diversity, adults can expect youth to demonstrate different ways of being, doing, and acting. Students are fully human and in various stages of maturation, so sometimes they may not sit still, they may talk when they aren't holding the talking piece, or they may refuse to speak. Therefore, the Circle Keeper must be aware, actively involved in what is going on, and understanding about the various ideas and perspectives presented.

Students, like all people, will need to test whether there is trust in the Circle before they share, and while they are assessing, they may experience embarrassment and even want to project the embarrassment onto someone else. They may not be compassionate and may say something mean to someone in the Circle. This is when the Circle Keeper must remind them, when they get the talking piece, about the shared and agreed-upon guidelines and values. Another concern is that students may not take seriously that all Circle members must keep private all that is discussed in Circle. It is vital to emphasize that all participants must not talk to others outside the Circle about what has been shared in Circle, and to discuss together during the guidelines round why privacy is so important. It may happen that a participant reveals information to someone who wasn't part of the Circle. At the next meeting, the Circle will have to decide together what to do about that, make and reaffirm agreements, and follow through and follow up.

Keep in mind that no matter how well developed tier 1 community-building and Circle processes are, the lives of all participants are not simple and may be quite complicated. They may have adult responsibilities and cares related to their families and communities. These relationships influence the way that each person participates in the classroom community, with each likely bringing different expectations and understandings about how to relate to others.

Another important factor for classroom dynamics and community building pertains to the impact of trauma on the students' social and emotional selves and active development of their brains. As already mentioned, early adverse childhood experiences affect the brains and bodies of young people in such a way that learning, being in a classroom, and sitting may be unusually challenging for some. When you have more than a couple of students suffering complex trauma, it's probable that there is an entanglement of unmet needs among the various players in the classroom. To be trauma-informed and to practice trauma-sensitive ways in the classroom is critically necessary for the well-being of all.

Connecting Circles to ELA Classrooms

Once students understand the various elements of Circle practice and get to know each other through a Relationship-Building Circle, English teachers can integrate these same elements into their curriculum. For example, teachers might open and close the class with a quote, a poem, or a song written by a published author or by a student that connects to a book or theme the class is studying. Or the students together might create a centerpiece or talking piece that reflects an important image or metaphor from a book, story, or poem. ELA teachers can integrate reading and writing throughout the Circle process, especially by posing and responding to questions. For example, you might try co-creating the goals of Community-Building Circles and the ELA curriculum by posing questions to your students using the guide in Figure 2.11 as a means to initiate these conversations. (For more specifics on how ELA teachers might use Circles, see Chapter 5.)

Tier 2: Repairing Relationships

With a strong, proactive tier 1 foundation in place, this next tier supports students in learning that when they experience or cause harm, it affects many people directly and indirectly. The grounding in relationships, accomplished in tier 1, provides the human and social capital for processing conflict and intervening to stop or prevent harm, which happens in tier 2 of the whole-school model of restorative justice in education (see Figure 2.4). Although tier 2 practices are best led by trained leaders, we offer here a brief look at the purposes and impact of this tier.

When unmet needs contribute to a conflict, RJE sees an opportunity for the expression of those needs in a structured conference led by a trained RJE facilitator. Such unmet needs may have roots in the young person's past, and it may not be possible to address or fulfill those needs in the classroom context. Additionally, there may be current circumstances, including within the classroom, that are a factor in unmet needs. Teachers may be invited to participate in a Repairing Relationships Circle and in discipline conferences. Participants involved in a conflict are invited to meet together, process the situation, and agree on actions that heal the harm done to the relationship by the conflict. Repairing Relationships Circles and discipline conferences reframe the situation to acknowledge the harm caused to relationships, rather than focus on rule breaking and punishment. They handle situations that might ordinarily be referred to an administrator to consider for an out-of-class or school suspension.

Why the emphasis on harm? One of the principles of RJE is that when a rule is broken, the impact on the relationships of the people affected is of primary concern. When schools understand and honor this concept, they change how they view and relate to students, as well as how they perceive rule breaking. They move away from punishment and instead attend to the unmet need(s) that the student or students are expressing by breaking a rule.

If schools are to move toward being restorative, they have to reevaluate their disciplinary practices. First, schools need to change their disciplinary lens from focusing only on the student who *caused* the harm to attending to the person who *was* harmed: asking them about the hurt or harm they have experienced, how they were hurt, and what they need in order to heal from the harm. Second, schools can begin to notice how the community and people who are associated with the person who was harmed also have been affected by the harm. Third, schools can see the person who behaved "badly" as someone in need of teaching and healing. RJE helps us see that there may be an underlying reason why the student did what they did; finding out what that is can be helpful in the healing process.

The cornerstones of RJE include collaboration guided by pro-social values; decision by consensus; healing the imbalance in the people directly affected by the wrongdoing; understanding the underlying reasons why someone harms another; and involving the community in the healing process. For teachers to engage with and be sensitive to the activities and understandings described here, they may need to examine their classroom practices and relational interactions both inside and outside of Circle processes with regard to inclusion, processes we explore in more depth in Chapters 3 and 4.

Tier 3: Reentry and Reintegration

Tier 3 practices of the whole-school model of restorative justice in education (Figure 2.4) also rely on facilitation by trained RJ practitioners to help students work through even more intense conflicts, including reentry and reintegration when they have been excluded from the classroom or school. The specific practices at this level include Repair Relationships Circles, if these were not facilitated before the student was excluded, and specifically the practices of a Reentry and Reintegration Circle. These practices work toward the goal of successful reentry when a student is genuinely welcomed back. Specific practices include reminding students to take responsibility for their actions, ensuring they are aware of the impact of their actions on others, and, with adult assistance, reintegrating them into the classroom and school community. It is vital that the Circle provide resources to help students succeed.

When students who have been suspended or expelled return to school, they face many challenges. They have to figure out how to become a part of the community that recently excluded them, both in the school and in the classroom. Other students may tease and ridicule them or target them in other ways. They may still harbor ill feelings toward others who may have been involved in the reason for their exclusion. They missed instruction and may already be falling behind, and the suspension may have exacerbated an already problematic academic situation. If students have not accepted their responsibility in the wrongdoing, they may still be blaming others for their predicament. They may also experience shame about facing their peers.

When we are cognizant of all the feelings that returning students may be experiencing, we can attend to their needs and thus avoid any additional barriers to their integration. One of the most important questions we work with in the Repair Relationships Circle is about identifying the underlying causes for the wrongdoing. Many times responses to this question allow others in the Circle to develop a deeper understanding of and compassion for the returning student. The student and his or her family may be suffering from physical, mental, or emotional problems that are preventing the student from succeeding at school. There is a host of difficult personal, familial needs and societal discrimination that can prevent a student from doing what is needed to succeed in school.

As stated earlier, societal injustices and inequities affect our students and their families deeply, and they need assistance to be able to extract themselves from the seemingly hopeless situations of poverty and other personal, familial, group, and intergenerational traumas. The stories we sometimes hear in Circle are painful and devastating. And in many instances, our educational and social services are not set up to provide adequate resources for all families. Many students have to shoulder adult responsibilities so that their families can survive. If they are an older sibling, they may have to care for younger sisters and brothers. When we have provided reentry and support Circles, we've discovered that many students who were tardy or had poor attendance did not have basic resources such as bus fare or an alarm clock to wake them up in the morning.

The reentry process allows the adults in the school to listen and figure out what can be provided for students so they can succeed. If the reentry process is handled in a sensitive and empathetic way, students will learn from their mistakes, and many students do not repeat their wrongdoings after going through such a process. They will be required in their Repair Relationships Circle to make amends. And when school personnel can assist them in doing so, everyone is able to heal. Having assigned adults do check-ins and check-outs of students who are reentering helps these students accept their responsibilities and step up to the challenges.

It may not always be easy to genuinely welcome a student back into the school community or into your classroom. This student may have caused harm and disruption in your class or been rude and disrespectful. He or she may have made it difficult for you to teach and facilitate learning in your classroom. This student may have tested your patience and required more care and energy than you were able to expend. Self-care and support from your colleagues is crucial if you are to be successful in reintegrating the student into the classroom. However, as the adult and the teacher in this case, you share the responsibility of reintegration with the student. However difficult it may be for you personally, you have to find a way to both take care of yourself and fully accept the student back into your classroom. If the Repairing Relationship Circle wasn't held before exclusion, then it must be implemented on the student's reentry if you and the student are to forge a healthier relationship with each other.

The Importance of Coordination and Follow-Through

Tier 3 and reentry require a strong collaboration among service providers and school personnel to make sure that the student receives sufficient services and support to do better in school and class. In many schools and districts, such services are duplicated or unorganized, preventing the smooth coordination of the various service providers. When a coordinator is assigned to manage the reentry plan, all parties do a better job of following through on the promises and agreements made in the reentry Circle. It also signals to students that they are cared for and belong in this community. Even with support, students may need more than one Circle to fully reintegrate.

Bringing Tiers Together: Reaffirming, Repairing, and Rebuilding Relationships

The most important tier for you as a teacher to attend to is tier 1, the daily relational practices that are grounded in pro-social values that reassure every child and adult that they are worthy, that they have dignity, and that their community wants and needs them. When tier 1 is well developed, fewer conflicts rise up in tiers 2 and 3. Without a strong tier 1, reentry is almost impossible. Tier 1 prevents more conflicts from occurring and promotes an ethos of acceptance and understanding of students who are returning after making and then learning from their mistakes. If not properly welcomed back, students remain at the margins of the educational community and find themselves unable to experience a sense of belonging, a paramount reason why students drop out or end up causing grievous harm to themselves or others.

RJE encourages us to think about conflict in new ways. What happens if we consider conflict as an opportunity and a gift to deepen relationships, rather than as an occasion to assign blame, which is the norm in too many schools? What if we peel back the underlying layers of conflict to find ways to help people heal and thus prevent another occurrence of the conflict? Without such gentle attendance to conflicts, many people become afraid of conflict and eventually become conflict-averse. When conflict has no way to be resolved, it festers and increases in intensity and complexity. RJE asks us to use better ways to deal with conflict: to slow things down, to sit down and have conversations about what happened, who got hurt, who will take responsibility, and how we can heal.

In the classroom, when restorative Community-Building Circles are held weekly or bimonthly, trust develops, and then issues related to conflicts can be broached as a community concern. Rather than blaming and shaming, we rely on the norms and values we established as a group to prevent and, if necessary, reduce the impact of conflict.

What can we do, however, if conflict does develop? For smaller or less intense conflicts that occur in the classroom, teachers can offer students a restorative conversation or a hallway conference. A restorative conversation is a one-on-one dialogue between teacher and student to slow things down when an incident is moving toward conflict or disagreement. It's an *informal* conversation using a set of questions to quickly assess any needs the student(s) may have, and then attend to those needs to prevent escalation into a more serious conflict and to prevent any harm. Restorative conversations make space for quickly processing a situation and responding to needs.

Beginning a Restorative Conversation

To begin a restorative conversation, quickly do the following:

1. **Assess your own readiness.**
   - to engage with the student and still maintain order in the classroom; and
   - to be curious about what happened this time rather than falling into "knowing" even before you hear what happened.

2. **Assess the student's readiness.**

   - What do you know about the particular student and his or her needs?

   - What do you know about the student's patterns of reactions?

   - Can you have a quick conversation to prevent or contain the harm and redirect, or will this take more time?

3. **Assess the context.**

   - Is this a good time?

   - How will the other students react?

   - Are there particular students who may react in a way that can make this a bigger issue?

   - Can you stop what is happening for now and make time after class or school to have a longer restorative conversation with the student?

   - Do you have the conversation inside the classroom or in the hallway? To do this, you may have to assess the hallway traffic.

After your assessment and if you are ready to have the conversation:

1. Invite the student to step out into the hallway or closer to you so you can have this conversation in privacy.

2. Let the student know you want to have a quick conversation about what is going on. (*Tommy, I would like to have a quick conversation with you about what's happening here.*)

3. Ask the student if he or she also wants to have a conversation about what's going on. (*Are you okay to have this conversation with me now?*) If "yes" continue; if "no," suggest another time to have the conversation.

4. If yes, begin by acknowledging something the student is doing well, then broach the subject about your concern. An example of the dialogue might be:

   - *I'm noticing that you're paying attention a lot more than you were two weeks ago. That is really great. And I did want to talk with you about [issue]. When I see you doing [issue], I am affected by [issue] and this is how it affects me—I get upset, irritated, anxious. I want to understand what's going on for you.*

   - Listen for what the student needs.

   - Use the questions below to get a greater understanding of why the student is acting the way he or she is. Allow the student to speak freely.

   - Explain what you need from the student.

- Assess whether the student can follow through with your direction.
- Offer help.
- Thank the student for having the conversation and repeat what he or she will do to settle the situation. And offer your assistance again.
- Don't forget to keep an eye on the rest of the students.
- Return to the whole class.

Guiding and Sample Questions for a Restorative Conversation

From the following guiding and sample questions, choose those that are the most relevant to your context and situation.

- What is happening/what happened?
- How did it happen?
- What were you thinking at that time?
- What were you feeling at that time?
- Was anyone hurt or harmed?
- Who do you think was affected?
- How were the others affected?
- What needs do they have because of the harm?
- What do you take responsibility for?
- What needs to happen to make things right?
- What would you like to offer and to whom?
- What do you need to be able to make amends?
- How can I help you?
- How are you doing now?

If you cannot resolve the issue, then you may have to request assistance to have a longer discussion with the student and a trained RJE facilitator. This situation may be more complicated than you originally thought. The RJE facilitator will follow the steps of a Repair Relationships Circle. This is when RJE should be implemented using a whole-school approach, so that everyone in the school understands and uses restorative practices.

Ultimately, the strength of the community determines the quality of relationships that affect the learning and teaching in schools. Teachers are important contributors to the peace within a school and to the community outside of the building. We are grateful to teachers and all the other school staff who sacrifice and are there for all of our children in schools. We depend heavily on community partners, school administrators, and district officials to become involved in the health of every student and every classroom by introducing and providing restorative justice practices in schools. Practitioners in restorative justice in education are always looking for ways to incorporate RJE practices and principles in core subject classrooms.

Many studies and research demonstrate the benefits of using RJE in classrooms and schools. Our youth and adults deserve a peaceful and thriving community. To make this happen, as one of the seven assumptions listed earlier states, "Everything we need to make positive change is already here." We have to turn to ourselves and one another to create communities of caring and, we would venture to say, love. Dr. Martin Luther King Jr. expressed the need for a "Beloved Community"; that is not a far-off dream—it can be experienced here in schools now. How can we create beloved communities in ELA classrooms specifically? In the following chapters, we discuss how to call students into community through literate avenues and pedagogical approaches.

Chapter Three

Using Our Curricular Powers: Pedagogy and Restoration in the ELA Classroom

What does the work of a restorative English language arts education consist of? In one sense, it is a new way of being in our classroom spaces: it seeks to foster understanding and community, build and reinforce relationships, and create places where all human beings are seen, heard, and valued. On the other hand, this work is not new at all: as Pranis (2005) reminds us, "[T]his new way is really very old. . . . It combines . . . ancient tradition with contemporary concepts of democracy and inclusivity in a complex, multicultural society" (p. 3). For many of us, the content and pedagogies of ELA classrooms seem a good fit for this approach, as we suggest in this chapter.

Let's begin by revisiting this notion we have discussed in the last two chapters: a restorative approach in the contemporary era of schooling must begin with an understanding that *attending and being in school has harmed and continues to harm many students*. Far too often, school is not a place where students come to learn; it is, especially for minoritized and marginalized youth, a place where they are sorted, labeled, and storied in deleterious ways. Learning and schooling are in diametric opposition for many of these students. Our American public school system, as it currently stands, leaves many students standing at the door of educational spaces and does not authentically invite them in.

From Circles to Curriculum: Integrating RJE Principles into Pedagogical Practice

In Chapter 2, we explored the roots of restorative justice in education: its history and principal values. We also began to explore the ways in which restorative justice can be manifested through the use of Circles, holistic spaces where individuals share of themselves, listen with intent, build community, and engage in dialogue. Through Circles that focus on building community, repairing relationships, and reintegrating students into schools, classrooms have the potential to become spaces of transformative and radical healing for both teachers and students. These transformative possibilities do not end with the Circle, however, because the work of an RJE classroom incorporates pedagogical manifestations of restoration within and outside of Circle spaces. Specifically, a restorative approach in English classrooms contests, alters, and strives to erase harmful schooling experiences by not only ensuring that students are demonstrably valued members of the learning community, but by doing so through the pedagogies and practices of the English language arts. A restorative approach in these settings requires extraordinary (com)passion, patience, and, above all, commitment to shaping our curriculum to meet students' needs *where they are, with love, and without judgment.* From this stance, students do not fit neatly into a preplanned ELA curriculum, with meaning already determined for them. Rather, students *are* the curriculum; they determine the utility of the literary tools and processes presented to them, thus disrupting the cycle of devaluing student perspectives and literacies we have discussed as often residing in (sometimes well-intentioned) schools, programs, curricula, and classrooms. Teachers in the restorative justice English classroom oversee the agential development of the young people in their care. Teachers call for and appreciate divergent viewpoints, use texts that draw from their students' lives, and create relational scaffolds necessary for carrying out literate work. Toward the goal of designing such a classroom space, in this chapter we address the following questions:

- What does pedagogy have to do with a restorative justice English education?
- What pedagogical and curricular tools can English teachers employ to encourage a restorative classroom context?

In this chapter, we seek to bridge the work of a restorative justice English education and curriculum by articulating specific ways relationships can be reaffirmed, repaired, and rebuilt through pedagogical and literacy-oriented avenues. Maisha has stated in her work that English teachers can use their "curricular powers" to create a classroom space where youth "engag[e] in deliberate literate acts that illuminate pathways of resistance" (Winn, 2013, p. 127). In the English classroom, incorporating pedagogical approaches that counteract institutional and interpersonal harm; engaging students' experiences, lives, and opinions as integral components of classroom work; and opening avenues for critical reflection and resistance are paramount to materializing a restorative space. In such a classroom, as we introduced in Chapters 1 and 2, the goals are to foster relationship building, disrupt monolithic lenses, and open spaces for student voice, pathways, and experience.

More than anything, we believe that employing a restorative approach necessitates articulating and personifying a restorative mindset. We also recognize that mindsets do not occur without action, and models of curricular and pedagogical approaches are essential for building a restorative culture. Thus, in this chapter we offer four pedagogical approaches with corresponding tools we view as fundamental to building a restorative English classroom space:

1. **Fashioning inclusive contexts** in which student responses to texts are *always* valued and seen as a learning tool, and in doing so *restoring and restorying* the way *all* student contributions can assist in making sense of texts

2. **Integrating "lived" literate materials** as a regular component of the curriculum *in addition to* offering a rich, diverse array of books and texts that reflect a "windows and mirrors" approach

3. **Creating a dialogic classroom that values alternative viewpoints** and regularly provides opportunities (preplanned and spontaneous) for students and teacher to collaborate in meaning-making

4. **Engaging in emancipatory literacies that develop a critical, action-oriented consciousness** through evoking and introducing multiple perspectives on texts and topics and helping students consider how they might alleviate inequity

All four of these, while listed independently, work in tandem with one another. They also work in tandem with Circle practices. As pedagogical *approaches*, they act as flexible, context-driven means to address the work of the English classroom in ways that call students in—their lives, experiences, and values. Asking students to share themselves does not end with a Circle; creating a classroom environment in which students are taken seriously as meaning-makers and literate experts invites continuous space for community building, restoration, and learning.

We also wish to underscore that it is possible and necessary to engage these components alongside the Common Core State Standards and other state and local standards. We see this work as a continuum; a healthy classroom culture and community is imperative for all learning and learners. It is impossible to nurture a critical mindset or create a dialogue-rich classroom in an educational space where students' responses are not valued, and vice versa. And, while the list of practices enumerated in this chapter are interdependent, they are also not exhaustive. A restorative classroom cannot be confined to a prespecified set of curricular principles or pedagogic techniques; above all else, this approach requires *creativity*, *reflection*, and *love*. Keeping these commitments in mind, we offer introductory ways to open the classroom door to all students, especially those who have been left standing in its entryway.

Opening the Door: Curricular and Pedagogical Approaches That Call Students In

1. Fashioning Inclusive Contexts: Restoring and Restorying

One of the reasons we became English teachers and restorative practitioners was because we loved stories—telling them, listening to them, discussing them with friends. In Chapter 1, we discussed the narratives that kept us spellbound in our youth. As adults, we are still spellbound by stories. Throughout the week, Hannah listens to a revolving door of narrative-format podcasts, even going so far as to install a radio in the shower. Maisha grew up in a family in which one had to engage in storytelling and endure being the center of stories with all of the wit one could muster. Rita was raised in a diverse community in Singapore where the ritual of eating, drinking tea, and sharing stories was an integral component of everyday life and constituted the fabric of family interactions.

As English educators and practitioners who work with English educators, we understand the incredible power that narrative holds to shape our lives and determine our outlook on the world. This power contains great promise and peril, as stories can be used to empower or suppress, inspire or destroy. Chapter 1 of this book reminds us of the powerful ways in which stories of literacy and of who is or deserves to be seen as literate have been deeply ingrained in our psyches. Author Chimamanda Ngozi Adichie's popular TED Talk (2009) on the "dangers of a single story" is a compelling reminder of the command that narrative holds in society, stating that all of us are "impressionable and vulnerable . . . in the face of a story, particularly as children." Adichie reminds us that stories themselves can concretize or disrupt histories, determine whose story is "correct," and who is worthy of having their story told.

Using stories to educate is often the primary method of English educators, who have historically been appointed the task of illuminating meaning for young people. Pertaining to the broader work of the English classroom, the notion of "story" in this sense is twofold: stories as literary accounts *and* as the way students are positioned as learners, experts, and class contributors. In her work researching more than a hundred years of reading comprehension research and testing in the United States, Willis (2008) traces how textual meaning has been used as a tool to highlight the intelligence of a select few and disparage the aptitude of others, noting: "Too often racism and classism are undercurrents that flow beneath the surface of reading comprehension research and testing where children of color are used as fodder to bolster claims of White children's intellectual superiority" (xxxi). These undercurrents are reflected *in and by* the curriculum taught in classrooms, including English classrooms. The notion that some readers' interpretations of a text are worthier than others is itself a *story*, a narrative that has been systematically dispersed over decades through narrow conceptualizations of what constitutes the canon of great literature and declarations of certain interpretations of texts as definitive. Such a story redounds to the benefit of a select few, and the divisions this approach creates are unmistakably demarcated along racial, linguistic, and socioeconomic lines (Greene, 2008; Gutiérrez et al., 2002; Lee, 1998; Shannon, 1998). The question for teachers, then, is this: What strategies can help us combat the "single stories" of textual meaning and interpretation in the classroom by creating spaces of communal learning and collaboration in English classrooms?

When we as teachers begin to think deeply about the origins of meaning and whose narratives, backgrounds, and interpretations matter in schools, we start to understand how limiting has been an approach that considers only dominant narratives. To resolve the negative outcomes of this more traditional method of teaching, in which teachers (and other experts) hold knowledge and students are considered to have little or none, the conversation must turn from one in which we as English educators ask, *How can I make sure my students understand this text?*, to one that implores us to inquire, *What does this text mean to and for my students?* and *What does this material do for my students?* From this standpoint, the litmus test of an English curriculum is not whether students *get it*, but rather what they think about it, how or if it matters to them, and how it assists them in achieving their goals.

Many educators support the principle that student interpretation should be valued. Most of us actively encourage interpretation in our lessons; we excitedly ask students to draw parallels between the text and their lives, have them "translate" the text into their own words, or invite them to articulate their take on the motivations of characters or salient themes or authorial intentions, etc. While these are important, commendable activities, we must also force ourselves to confront the bias in our evaluation of student interpretation. Nearly all of us—particularly those of us with advanced degrees in English—have been acculturated to believe that there are at least *some* defensible truths associated with textual interpretation. For instance, we may strongly believe that textual analysis begins with understanding what the text actually "says." Such beliefs, however, are often the breeding ground of single stories about whose interpretation "counts" in classrooms (Lewis, 1993), as it suggests that what a text "says" is a neutral act of comprehension. Believing that reading and interpreting a text is purely a replicable act of decoding and comprehending may cause us to devalue student interpretations that don't fit with our preconfigured understanding of a text, so we offer only interpretations that do. Restorative classrooms reorient and restory these spaces to value the multiple interpretations and capacity for understanding that many youth, particularly youth of color and English language learners, are often denied in English classrooms. By *restory*, we mean valuing and promoting the interpretations of all students, thus "reshaping narratives to better reflect a diversity of perspectives and experiences" (Thomas & Stornaiuolo, 2016, p. 314) and actively constructing positive learner identities (Worthy, Consalvo, Bogard, & Russell, 2012). The process of reshaping narratives dovetails with the tier 1 work of restorative justice in education, discussed in detail in Chapter 2, of building community and creating space for multiple voices as part of a holistic RJE approach.

Part of creating and reshaping narratives in classrooms means accepting responsibility for the power that we as educators hold in creating spaces where students in our care feel that their ideas, opinions, and personhood are valued. In a study examining students' perceptions of teacher personalism, Phillippo (2012) found that while students' perceptions of teacher trustworthiness were affected by direct (personal) interactions, *observed* interactions were highly important factors in building trusting relationships. Just like adults, young people are constantly "sizing up" the grown-ups that surround them, determining who will support them and who might deprecate them. We know from experience and decades of research that students do better academically, emotionally, and socially in classrooms where their ideas, personhood, background, and whole selves are cherished, nurtured, and encouraged. Such classrooms often embolden students to possess what Johnston (2012) refers to as a *dynamic learning* frame, through which intelligence is viewed as process oriented and collaborative. A dynamic learning frame stands in opposition to a *fixed-performance* learning frame, through which intelligence is seen as stationary, competitive, and something a person either has or doesn't have. The way in which teachers set up their classrooms and respond to students is a major determinant of how students understand knowledge, intelligence, and learning in the classroom, as "surprisingly small changes in feedback can have quite broad consequences, because the feedback marks whether we are in the fixed-performance world or the dynamic-learning world" (Johnston, 2012, p. 39). Teachers who encourage students to depend on validation of their intelligence through public confirmation of "correct" responses (even if that validation is positively framed) may encourage a fixed-performance mindset, fostering a "single story" classroom space where students are reticent about sharing their perspectives for fear of not being right.

So, how does this connect to the ELA classroom? While there is no clear road map for demonstrably valuing and encouraging all student interpretations, there are ways to begin creating an English classroom in which students feel that they and their responses are integral. See the following In Practice suggestions and classroom vignette for ideas to get you started.

In Practice . . .

- **Create the space for students to have real, interpretative, imaginative responses to texts.** While this might seem obvious, think carefully about your current classroom, curriculum, and school environment. With ever-increasing concern surrounding standardized test scores and a subsequent adherence to prepackaged curricula, textbooks, and objectives, eliciting student responses for the purpose of exploring alternative interpretations (and multiple stories) of a text may be rare, even though reader response has been well documented as a fundamental way people read and make sense of texts (Rosenblatt, 1994). Ensure you are creating space for students to authentically share divergent and imaginative analyses through questions, writing, and classroom activities that call for and rely on student input (see features of Cory's example in the following vignette). For example, rather than solely or initially asking comprehension questions about a text, ask questions about student responses, reactions, and thoughts emerging from the experience. Beginning with something as simple as *What did you think of this?*, *What did you take from this?* or *What are you thinking about now?* allows conversations to evolve among students organically, creating an atmosphere in which varied ideas and opinions are more likely to emerge.

- **Affirm student responses to a text, even if—and especially when— their responses don't agree with "common" (or your personal) understandings of the text.** This can be difficult, particularly when student interpretations seem radically different from what the text seemingly conveys. Rather than dismissing divergent interpretations out of hand, however, give students space to explain their thoughts and encourage group discussion. Encouraging students to share their personal textual interpretations can lead to transformational conversations among students that uncover new possibilities for meaning (Aukerman, 2013) while transforming the classroom into a place where interpretation is never static, but always part of a personal and contextualized reading. *Affirm* and *encourage* in this sense do not necessarily mean "praise"—they mean that you, the teacher, accept all student input and interpretations as *legitimate and worthy* in the classroom space. One way of doing this is to begin taking a backseat in these discussions; rather than responding to every student's input, encourage others to speak back to one another and grapple with the complex task of making meaning. This encourages all students to share and give their input, including those who might be nervous to speak up for (often historically grounded) fear of being dismissed.

- **Encourage a dynamic learning frame in your classroom.** Focus feedback on strategy, effect, and thought processes rather than on your personal verification or dissent surrounding student input. For example, rather than telling students that their response is "good" or "not on the mark," encourage them to explain their thinking, ask other students to share their thoughts in response, explain what their response made you think about, or offer your thinking as a possible alternative (rather than the definitive answer). Implementing a dynamic learning frame also coincides with creating a dialogic classroom space, discussed further in this chapter.

Into the Classroom: Approaching Restorying

Cory Foxen, grades 9–12 English teacher

The more I think about English classrooms and social justice, the more solidified I become in my thinking that secondary English classrooms are not—and should not be—spaces solely for the production of reading and writing activities done in order to please the teacher. Valuable opportunities lie in the secondary English classroom for personal growth, communal understanding, and the development of one's ability to answer larger questions about society and inequality through literate avenues. As an educator of young people, I believe we must remain focused, intentional, and dedicated to social justice, which includes the restorying of students in relation to school "work."

An important part of restorying in my classroom consists of creating opportunities for all students to feel that they have valuable contributions to share in connection with reading and writing activities. For example, this past year one of my students had frequent contact with law enforcement and was eventually expelled from school. When he came to my class in an alternative high school program, he felt as though his academic life was over. Initially, he didn't want to choose a book to read for the quarter, he didn't want to respond to our daily writing prompts, and he didn't want to share in class. It would have been easy, as a teacher, to simply throw up my hands and believe that he refused to engage. Instead, I didn't see him as refusing, but as hesitant; I saw him as a student whose connection with school and the work of English class had the potential to be restoried.

I decided to talk to this student and find out how he felt about school and English class. Through our conversations, it became clear that his hesitancies were indicative of deeper concerns and fears. Previous schools and teachers had labeled him as aggressive, disrespectful, and unwilling to engage in class. He shared with me that he was not unwilling to engage; rather, he just didn't want to engage with teachers who seemed to think he was unwilling or incapable of doing more than the bare minimum.

If we are to foster a community in our classrooms that is constantly seeking to restory, we have to position all students as not only capable, but also as indispensably valued members of a literary community. I wanted to create space for this student to evolve, grow, and be a valued intellectual. I wanted to work with him and hear about his interests and ideas, rather than telling him what to read and write. I decided to demonstrably value his opinions by creating open reading and writing assignments aimed at restorying both his academic potential and what "counted" as a classroom text and class work. For example, in speaking to this student and others in my class, I found that many had a deep interest in and love for hip-hop. Each day during the daily writing prompt, I built on that interest by playing hip-hop instrumentals that served as background music. When I read through their writing notebooks, I noticed a change in their writing responses. Students who rarely wrote more than a sentence or two were writing a page or more in the form of hip-hop verses (similar to stanzas of poetry) that matched the instrumental playing. The student who prompted this change frequently wrote hip-hop verses and would occasionally perform them for the class. In addition to the immediate impact on community building, these moments laid the foundation for the restorying of this student.

On several occasions, we wound up dropping the writing prompt altogether and held a cypher. A cypher is a group of people gathered, typically in a circle, to rap. Oftentimes, one person's rhymes would piggyback off of someone else's in order to maintain the topic of the prompt. It would start with a student freestyling in response to the prompt, and then we segued into our own version of Sway's "Five Fingers of Death." The "Five Fingers of Death" is a segment on Sway's radio show where he invites hip-hop artists to freestyle to five different instrumentals. Similar to musical chairs, the artist doesn't know when the instrumental will change and has to adapt the rhyme scheme when it does. In addition to the music changing, Sway throws out a topic that the artist needs to touch on and incorporate into his or her lyrics. A cypher is seen as a rite of passage by many in the hip-hop community because of how skilled an artist has to be to do it.

This particular student was already a skilled writer-poet, but these cyphers gave him a chance to truly shine and connect. His quick wit, authority in speaking and engaging the room, and grasp of language was highlighted in these moments. This student, who at first rarely responded to the writing prompts or shared his thoughts, began to engage in class in new and exciting ways. He began to see himself as a part of the classroom, as someone with worthy skills, ideas, and opinions to contribute. When different topics were thrown out during the cypher, I wasn't the only one changing the topic—other students also threw out new topics. This further reinforced what I continued to tell and show my students: I do not hold all of the knowledge in this class, and my ideas are not the most important. We are a community, and communities thrive, grow, and learn through collaboration. This messaging, apparent throughout the course, deeply affected how my students understood the purpose and concerns of school and our English classroom. The messaging affirmed that they were central to the process of schooling: their ideas mattered.

As his time with us was coming to an end with the end of the semester, the student had concerns about his life after he left our program. He didn't want to leave a place that was supportive of him in exchange for a place that didn't even want him in the building. Because he had missed a lot of school, he wasn't making progress on his final project (a comparative analysis of two songs discussed in *The Rap Year Book* by Shea Serrano)—at least not tangible progress. Why do I say "tangible"? Because educators are often singularly focused on what we can see students produce, which ignores what students are really doing. We don't always pause to embrace the process. With a week and a half left before his project was due, the student came to me and told me he hadn't done any work on it in weeks and didn't think he would be able to get it done in time. Rather than force him to turn in something he wouldn't be able to do and set this student up for possible failure, I asked him if he would like to amend the project. My suggestion: show me a piece of you that you want me to see. No parameters. No guidelines.

On the final day of the semester, the day the project was due, the student turned in a single college-ruled piece of paper. Written on it was a poem. The top half of the piece was titled "The Good"; the bottom half was titled "The Bad." As I read through it, I could see the student's thought process unfolding in front of me, quite literally. There were scribbled-out words and phrases, as the edits barely fit in the margins. The poem was a conversation with himself. He addressed his good nature and his bad nature. He explored the reasons for several of the choices that had led up to his expulsion. He questioned some of his habits. In many ways, the poem was a comparative analysis of himself.

Although the tangible product was not what I had anticipated, the outcome was exactly what I had hoped for. The student was wrestling with ideas, seeking to understand himself in a deeper, more nuanced way. Because our classroom was a space where his thoughts and writings had been affirmed as valuable, he felt comfortable showing me how they played out simultaneously. What I received was a prime example of how the community we as educators establish, and the things we choose to affirm in our community, have a major impact on the processes our students choose to engage with. Restorying students starts with the choices educators make about the purpose of education, and how to call all students into the learning process.

2. Integrating Lived Literate Materials: Windows, Mirrors, and Beyond

For decades there has been a call for the books that line bookstore and classroom shelves to reflect the real diversity of American children, families, and neighborhoods. Recent, powerful grassroots movements such as We Need Diverse Books and #1000blackgirlbooks have pushed for texts that highlight experiences and perspectives outside the all-too-familiar purview of White, middle-class, ablest, heterosexual, and cisgendered characters and authors. Researchers have long written about the deeply problematic nature of texts in classrooms that reflect only a small subsection of the American populace; unfortunately, the lack of diversity in children's and young adult literature is an ongoing problem.[11] For students who fall outside the parameters of the group most literature focuses on, there is a risk of feeling disconnected and marginalized. At the same time, those children who *do* see themselves constantly reflected in books may experience a disconnect between

Resource Spotlight: Reflecting and Discovering Lives

Windows and Mirrors

Collier, Lorna. "No Longer Invisible: How Diverse Literature Helps Children Find Themselves in Books, and Why It Matters." *The Council Chronicle, September 2016*. Retrieved from http://www.ncte.org/library/NCTEFiles/Resources/Journals/CC/0261-sept2016/NoLongerInvisible.pdf (see the "Resources for Teachers Seeking to Use More Diverse Texts" sidebar)

Cooperative Children's Book Center at the University of Wisconsin–Madison: https://ccbc.education.wisc.edu/default.asp

Diversity in YA on Tumblr: http://diversityinya.tumblr.com/

Weneediversebooks Campaign: http://weneeddiversebooks.org/where-to-find-diverse-books/

. . . And Beyond

Christensen, Linda. *Teaching for Joy and Justice: Re-imagining the Language Arts Classroom.* Milwaukee: Rethinking Schools, 2009.

González, Norma, Luis C. Moll, and Cathy Amanti, eds. *Funds of Knowledge: Theorizing Practices in Households, Communities, and Classrooms.* Mahwah, NJ: Erlbaum, 2005.

Paris, Django, and H. Samy Alim, eds. *Culturally Sustaining Pedagogies: Teaching and Learning for Justice in a Changing World.* New York: Teachers College Press, 2017.

the real diversity of the world and their place in it. As Bishop (1990) notes, children who see only "reflections of themselves . . . will grow up with an exaggerated sense of their own importance and value in the world—a dangerous ethnocentrism" (p. ix). The need for our selection of books to take into consideration the many ways that youth exist in the world while providing inroads toward understanding others' experiences has been referred to as providing "windows and mirrors" (Bishop, 1990) for young people: mirrors that reflect students' experiences and windows that provide insight into the experiences of others.

In the restorative justice English education classroom, texts are fertile ground for building relationships, restoring peace, repairing harm, and working toward understanding oneself and others. Windows and mirrors are essential tools in this process. However, they are still teacher-curated tools that cannot represent the complete breadth of experiences in the classroom or world. To more fully draw on the classroom community's literate and sense-making assets, teachers can work to incorporate "lived" literate experiences: those cultural processes and tools students and their communities draw on in their everyday lives to read, write, and make sense of the world. These literate experiences are both the material ways in which students communicate with family and friends and the immaterial ways in which young people make sense of those communications. These tools include memories, ideas, and thoughts that guide students in interpreting the world around them. In the restorative English classroom, the sense-making tools of experience, opinion, and memory are centered. When these processes and tools are seen as an integral component of learning and woven into the curriculum, students' lives and the work of the English class become intertwined.

So how do we get there? Asking students to bring in their literate, social, and emotional lives is not something that happens instantaneously. Students need to trust that what they bring in will be valued and accepted, the cornerstone of a restorative space (see the previous section). Once these foundations are in place, possibilities for learning and exploring grow. For example, Hannah recently worked with a preservice teacher who wanted to build a classroom space in which multiple perspectives and literate practices were validated, encouraged, and examined. This teacher began by capitalizing on her students' text messaging expertise, an everyday literacy tool her students were engaged in (similar to the work being done in Carla's class, highlighted in the vignette on pp. 56–57). This teacher candidate chose to view texting as an opportunity to collaboratively explore the difference between spoken and written dialogue. The consequence was that students leapt at the opportunity to integrate their personal, *textual* lives into the work of the classroom. This was more than a "hook"; these students were learning that their lives (and language) mattered in the context of the classroom and were part of the work of the English curriculum.

In Practice . . .

- Use every opportunity (creatively!) to engage student stories, literacies, and textual resources by:

  - **Building on cultural and personal attributes, assets, and interests you know your students engage in (mirrors).** Bring in literary material that reflects a component of your students' lives and encourage them to respond based on their experiences. For instance, if you know one or more students have a particular interest in a local or national issue, bring in news articles, texts, and resources that directly connect to this concern.

  - **Engaging students' literate experiences and knowledge.** Extending the concept of "mirrors" beyond texts also means building on your students' funds of knowledge (Moll, Amanti, Neff, & Gonzalez, 1992), literate and cultural practices, and everyday interpretations in the classroom. Find out what kind of texts students are actively engaged in (whether online, IRL [in real life], or throughout the course of their daily experiences), what interpretative gifts they bring, and what their everyday lives are filled with. Find ways at all turns—as the two teachers in the following vignettes demonstrate—to build from and with these experiences, making students' textual, relational, and interpretative lives integral to the work of the class.

- ○ **Building in space for students to tell stories in response to characters and narratives in texts that provide (or are positioned as providing) insight into others' experiences (windows).** Ask students to critique and respond to story lines, and in the process encourage them to articulate how these responses reflect and do not reflect their lives and experiences. This approach encourages students to think deeply about how characters/people are positioned in the texts they read, what might be missing, and what possible insight this reading gives them into another's experience of the world (including the author's) and/or society as a whole.

- Through the course of engaging in these approaches, **be extraordinarily careful not to undo the work of valuing student lives, literacies, interests, and interpretations by demarcating some texts, opinions, or practices as more commendable than others.** For instance, many teachers might try introducing a popular contemporary song as a hook or entryway into studying a "classic" short story or novel. However, we need to consider that this move could be viewed by students as a commentary on the value of the song, i.e., that it's not a *real* text worthy of consideration. It's vital that students' backgrounds, interests, and cultures—particularly those of students and communities of color—be sustained (Paris, 2012) in school settings; this can happen only when materials from students' lives are authentically seen, utilized, and presented as scholarly texts in their own right rather than solely as introductions to other material.

Into the Classroom: Integrating "Lived" Experiences

Carla Oppenheimer, grade 10 English teacher

In my classroom, I have found that integrating students' experiences and funds of knowledge has power and relevance beyond relating to the themes or characters in a text. Early in the year, in a lesson on what we mean by conventions of writing in the English classroom, I invited students to teach me about the conventions of twenty-first-century media. I began with a true story about how I found out that my perfectly punctuated text messages might be considered rude by many millennials, after I read a blog post about how a period at the end of a text can signify finality or impatience. The story got a lot of laughs, and by exposing myself as an English teacher who doesn't know everything, while simultaneously positioning reading and writing as a constantly in-flux social tool, I made space for students to become the experts. I followed up by asking students for their advice on how to improve my texts. They were delighted to make "what to do" and "what not to do" lists for texting and for Snapchat, another social media platform they use frequently. They debated and covered an impressive array of unspoken rules, from when to use all caps and periods to the maximum socially acceptable time to wait before replying to a text. They also taught me some technical vocabulary, such as *streaks* and *your story* on Snapchat. I have gotten enormous mileage out of this activity by building on it throughout the year, reinforcing the idea that conventions are context dependent as we encounter and produce different genres and styles of writing in our class.

For example, when we studied *Othello* later in the year, we compared the conventions of a play with the conventions for Snapchat streaks—a streak is made up of individual snaps back and forth, each of which consists of images or videos and a caption, just like a play is made up of scenes, each consisting of lines spoken by characters and stage directions. The comparison helped students see connections between their daily literate practices and a new convention, and when we practiced finding specific lines in their copies of the play they were excited to crack the code of act number, scene number, line number. Similarly, on another day, when we were studying narrative writing, I asked students to take out their phones and write down a brief text exchange. After a lesson on punctuating dialogue, I asked students to rewrite their text conversation as dialogue in a story to help them further examine convention differences in genres. These activities, done over the course of the school year, helped me to set the tone for my classroom community: it was a place where I expected students to bring their experiences and to have those become valued components of the curriculum. Even during that first discussion on twenty-first-century media, I noticed that all students contributed enthusiastically, including those who had previously been silent. Students picked up on my genuine excitement and joy at learning about their literacy practices—in my mind, I was just showing the same curiosity and respect in literacy that I expected from them—which led to students being more and more willing to offer their thoughts, experience, and noticings over the course of the year, aware that these contributions would be a valued part of our classroom space.

Into the Classroom: Integrating "Lived" Experiences

Julie Kesti, middle school ELA teacher

One thing I've experimented with this year is encouraging my sixth graders to be investigators of literate practices in their communities, asking them to bring their lives, interests, and opinions into the classroom while identifying and giving voice to the reading and writing lives of others. I've asked them to complete a series of interviews, starting informally with questions I generated and gradually moving into creating questions of their own and videotaping their interviews.

The early interviews required students to ask an older person about the most memorable books they'd ever read, how they feel about reading, what they'd read recently, and how they find things they like to read. The answers were recorded on paper. I asked students to work with someone older for these interviews in order to validate the natural mentors in their lives. Students may talk about literate practices with peers at school, but it's possible that this type of conversation remains separate from the rest of their lives. These interviews were informal and gave students a chance to become familiar with the interview process and how to ask someone to participate. Soon the behavior specialist downstairs and the security guard in our hall were sharing stories of childhood favorites and adult literacy practices like reading stacks of bills. Sometimes the adults were surprised to be asked these questions, but also happy to share their reflections with students and to be consulted as literacy experts. Students reached out to administration, elective teachers, cousins, siblings, and friends, some making more daring choices than others, but each coming back with stories to share.

The next set of interviews was again about reading, but the interviews were to be video-recorded. At first I added the video requirement to support students in their speaking and presenting abilities, but ultimately this format provided much more than that. Students asked interviewees how reading helps them in their daily life, when they've struggled or triumphed with reading, and what their life was like or would be like when or if they couldn't read. These interviews helped students think about the value of reading in new ways, created space for students to bring in others' lived experiences, and also helped me understand my students differently. Some students chose to work with teens from the connected high school, which intimidated them at first. I witnessed students' anxieties about talking to strangers and about getting older, and saw them proceed anyway and enjoy the work. The interview closed with the sixth graders asking the older students for advice. The advice they received was thoughtful and delivered with tender seriousness. Many of the older ELL students emphasized how recreational reading was crucial to their progress in English and school in general, but they also often added that they'd grown to love the way that reading helps them learn about the world. I saw my students take in this advice, and I also began to envision my students as future readers proud of their progress. Meanwhile, other students interviewed family members, giving me a glimpse of their sibling relationships, the things their parents are curious about, and the world inside their homes. These glimpses helped me to see my students more fully, giving me added context for understanding them and learning with them. It was illuminating to hear all about their mothers, sisters, and brothers, and to feel the humanity of these relationships that nurture my students outside of school.

Finally, I asked my students to design their own topics and questions for the last round of interviews. These interviews could be done with anyone and be edited together into a video essay with an introduction and a conclusion. Students were excited to begin. The assignment stated that the interviews needed to involve opinion and argument, but the topic choice was wide open. As they began to work, students came up to me every few minutes, cautiously asking, "I can ask about *anything*?" I responded affirmatively and reminded them of the basic requirements. They returned to their partners, sharing the exciting news that they could investigate *whatever they wanted*.

The topics they chose ranged from TV shows, sports teams, pets, K-pop, and ice cream to bullying, national politics, and the controversial show *13 Reasons Why*. The resulting list of topics was heavily reflective of their daily experiences—witnessing bullying, waking up too early, fangirling and eating school lunch. During the video-recording sessions, some of the most reticent students weren't shy at all about answering their classmates' questions—even when they were the only ones on camera. They liked having their opinion asked and having the power to disagree openly. They were being asked to discuss something they were an expert on: their opinions. This experience allowed students to learn about each other and themselves in new, exciting ways. One student, who rarely spoke in class, showed up in four other students' videos, growing bolder in expression and opinion each time. Another noted about conducting the interview: "Next time I won't be shy anymore. . . . It was interesting because some people have different thoughts on different things." Another student was pleased that the first two interviewees agreed with him about school lunch being terrible, but backed off his position slightly after a third student noted the importance of lunch to kids who don't have much food at home.

The final step in the opinion project was to edit everything together. Students' projects contained typical elements of a class essay—intro, body, and conclusion—but in a multimedia format. Students introduced their topics and their feelings about them, explored those of others, and summarized what they'd discovered and whether they'd changed their minds by the end. They tied it all together with images, video, and text. As they looked at a sample video I had made and viewed the progressing work of their classmates, I could see them making better sense of the purpose of an introduction and a conclusion (two of our academic goals associated with the unit), as well as starting to better grasp what made the videos stronger or weaker and why one might structure an argument in a particular way. There was also joy in their process. As they prepared their questions and started to figure out which classmates, family members, and friends would be good interview candidates for their topic, they turned to people around them as experts on literacy and meaning-making.

As we move into our next project—investigating a school rule and its merits—I continue to encourage students to flex these literacy skills of collection, exploration, and synthesis, acting as diligent investigators of the layered world around them, developing critical minds and using their voices, opinions, and experiences—as well as those of their families and communities—to do so.

3. Dialogic Teaching: Valuing Alternate Viewpoints in Action

It is difficult, if not impossible, to engage in the work of understanding ourselves, the world around us, and others if we do not find effective means of communicating. As English educators, our work is steeped in communication: finding and educating ourselves on various forms of it, studying it, and evoking it. This last is particularly important in a restorative English classroom, where student participation in educative work is a principal value.

Classrooms where ideas are freely shared, where students (and teacher) ask questions that provoke and sustain discussion, and where students are deeply interested in exploring concepts through communication are often referred to as *dialogic classrooms* exhibiting *dialogic teaching* techniques. Research shows that classrooms employing this approach assist students in seeing one another as resources for learning (Aukerman, 2012; Boyd & Markarian, 2011) and promote educational achievement (Nystrand, 1997).

Resource Spotlight: Encouraging and Reflecting on Classroom Dialogue

Alexander, Robin. *Towards Dialogic Teaching: Rethinking Classroom Talk*. Thirsk, UK: Dialogos, 2008.

Juzwik, Mary M., Carlin Borsheim-Black, Samantha Caughlan, and Anne Heintz. *Inspiring Dialogue: Talking to Learn in the English Classroom*. New York: Teachers College Press, 2013.

Mercer, Neil, and Steve Hodgkinson, eds. *Exploring Talk in Schools: Inspired by the Work of Douglas Barnes*. Los Angeles: SAGE, 2008.

Schultz, Katherine. *Rethinking Classroom Participation: Listening to Silent Voices*. New York: Teachers College Press, 2009.

In many ways, promoting a dialogic classroom encompasses features we have already discussed in relation to the restorative English classroom: a dialogic classroom demonstrably values student input and backgrounds. It encourages students to bring their interpretations (including—and especially—divergent analyses) to the classroom space, with these contributions becoming a core constituent of the curriculum. To create spaces in which student perspectives and opinions are valued as essential components, facilitating a dialogic classroom is imperative.

While research has revealed specific strategies teachers have employed to evoke discussion among students and teachers (see the Resource box opposite), here we offer introductory steps for facilitating meaningful interactions among students that encourage communication, consideration of alternative viewpoints, and joint meaning-making.

In Practice . . .

- **Incorporate multiple avenues for students to communicate and voice their opinions.** Not all students feel comfortable consistently sharing their insights verbally (initially or later in the year), even in restorative Circles. Rather than ask students to constantly engage in whole-class, small-group, or pair discussions, find alternative ways to involve students in sharing. Digital sites like Google Docs provide forays into co-journaling, while print journals that students create and pass around (with plenty of room for drawing as well as writing!) can create a community artifact of thoughts and insights. Other social media sites such as Twitter, Facebook Messenger, and Snapchat provide productive forums for communication. Employing multimodal products such as podcasts, infographics, and photograph-based narratives is another creative alternative. Find out which mediums your students use or prefer, and then work with these and build on them. Most important, integrate the options as legitimate means of expressing input; this requires creatively including such forums throughout the curriculum, and not just on special occasions.

- **Take note of your students' participation patterns.** Students participate in different ways and to varying degrees depending on the context, audience, and topic. Students who might be labeled as reticent or quiet in one class may come alive in another, while others might be more talkative depending on the subject at hand or the forum for communication. And, while participation has most often been equated with behavioral compliance, students are always participating in classrooms—just, perhaps, not always in the most desirable ways. Rather than force students to comply with our preferred method of participation, we suggest taking what Schultz (2009) refers to as an "inquiry stance toward silence" to closely examine classroom and individual patterns of participation. When students are silent, does their silence always mean they are disengaged? When do students seem to engage (both verbally and silently)? How can you build on these observations? Schultz explains that "listening for, inquiring into, and honoring silence might lead to louder, more dynamic, and engaged classrooms that have moments of silence where students pause for reflection. Most importantly, inquiry into classroom silence and participation might lead to classrooms where equitable participation is defined as broadly as possible" (p. 120). Classrooms where students and their various kinds of participation are considered worthy of thoughtful inquiry operate from a place of care and respect, a fundamental value of restorative justice.

- **Pay careful attention to what encourages thoughtful discussion in your classroom setting.** A wealth of research has determined that while often utilized, the initiate-respond-evaluate (IRE) sequence used in classrooms (a common situation in which a question is asked, a student responds, and the teacher publicly evaluates the response as acceptable or unacceptable) does not work effectively to promote extended, authentic discussion (Mehan, 1979; Nystrand, 1997). Rather, teachers must find ways to engage dialogic *stances* (Boyd & Markarian, 2011), in which dialogue is encouraged through thoughtful understanding of student participation practices and careful observation of what kinds of interactions foster discourse. Pay attention to what kinds of questions in your classroom seem to promote or diminish discussion among students, and what causes these discussions to build in the moment and over time. Although this may look different and work differently in every classroom, possible ideas for cultivating joint dialogue are:

  - Treat all ideas and responses as worthy of discussion (see Victor's classroom vignette on the following page)

  - When offering your opinion during class and small-group discussion, do so as a way to build bridges between ideas or make a genuine contribution to the conversation (rather than position your input as the correct one).

  - Cultivate a mindset whereby you, as the teacher, genuinely view discussions as ways to co-create knowledge and explore. Such a mindset is essential to achieving productive dialogue in the classroom.

Into the Classroom: Valuing Alternate Viewpoints in Action

Victor Johnson, grade 9 English teacher

While reading Elie Wiesel's *Night*, my class came upon a line in the book where Elie is reflecting on the incessant bells in the concentration camps that dictated his every move and, consequently, his ability to connect with his father, who was located in a different section of the camp. He wrote, "Whenever I dreamed of a better world, I could only imagine a universe with no bells." I asked my racially diverse students to think about something in the world that they saw as an injustice, and then asked for volunteers to complete the sentence, "Whenever I dream of a better world, I imagine a world without _____." A few students volunteered and we talked about their choices and what in their lives had led them to their choice. One student raised her hand and said, "Whenever I dream of a better world, I imagine a world without White people."

The classroom erupted. Some students became confrontational with this student, others supported her words, and even more drew in to themselves. If I had a different sense of what it meant to "manage" a classroom, I might have felt that I had completely lost control, and might have acted in a way that would have resulted in disciplining the student who caused the "disruption."

However, my goal as a teacher is not to discipline; it is to assist students' learning by valuing their words, their experiences, and the way they interact with and respond to a text. Was my student's reading of Elie Wiesel's reflection on a better universe not used as a frame for her own lived experience? Does the violence enacted on African American communities in the United States not parallel the experience of Elie Wiesel in twentieth-century Europe? Is there not a real anger around race relations in our country? To have disciplined in that moment, or to have changed the subject, would have been to negate that student's voice and her lived experience and, quite frankly, the idea that we can and must talk about the ugliness of our collective past and present if we are going to heal the sickness that is racism.

Following the student's statement, I dropped all of my plans for class that day in order to facilitate discussion around what had been said. We needed to hear what we all had to say. Students who were offended by their peer's words needed a space to talk, and students who understood her perspective needed a space to speak their truths. All was not fixed because of our conversation that day, but we did learn from each other's perspectives. When I think about what restorative justice can look like in an English classroom, I imagine and constantly try to create a space where the text, the plans for the day, and the notion of an "orderly" classroom that circumscribes confrontation will never supersede the needs, voices, and interpretations of my students.

4. Emancipatory Literacies: Developing a Critical, Action-Oriented Consciousness

A vital component of engaging in restorative justice work is appreciating justice as a process—a way of being heard, validated, and honored—rather than a solution.

Justice as a process entails a careful balance: it requires us to open our hearts and minds to other ways of being in the world, while simultaneously compelling us to repair unbalanced relationships that may be impeding a person's (or group's) liberation. The dual undertakings of *imagining alternative perspectives* and *acting to restore relationships* work as ethical markers in a space devoted to a restorative justice English education. These markers push us to consider how our pedagogical approach to engaging with texts reflects the values of a restorative education, the components of which we have begun to illuminate in this chapter.

In this final section on restorative approaches to the ELA classroom, we suggest that by its very nature, restorative work calls on educators to foster a critical consciousness in students and to provide actionable means for students to engage in critical work that is, at its core, a means for ratifying justice. To define *critical approaches*, we call on the theories of Paulo Freire (1973), who describes criticality as a product of understanding connectivity, since "the more accurately [people] grasp true causality, the more critical their understanding of reality will be" (p. 41). Moreover, with this understanding comes a yearning to alter, correct, and restore, as ultimately, "critical understanding leads to critical action" (p. 42). This call is also deeply resonant with Ladson-Billings's (1995) work on culturally relevant pedagogy, which—as a significant part of its concept—calls for the development of social critique, reminding us that "[n]ot only must teachers encourage academic success and cultural competence, they must help students to recognize, understand, and critique current social inequities" (p. 476).

There are decades of writing, research, and theorizing on how to incorporate critical practices into educational spaces. Integrating critical stances is, we argue, inherently and inextricably connected to the work of a restorative classroom space, and we urge you to read widely from illuminating examples, ideas, and theories of criticality in classroom spaces (see the Resource box on p. 70). With the philosophy of restorative justice in mind, we recommend taking the following (introductory) steps in English classroom spaces.

In Practice . . .

- **Draw on critical lenses as an authentic means to examine power and perspective in texts and contexts.** As we recognized earlier in this chapter, readers and contexts always shape the interpretation of texts. Staton (1987), quoted in Appleman (2015), explains that "each of us has a viewpoint invested with presuppositions about 'reality' and about ourselves, whether we are conscious of it or not. People who deny having a critical stance, who claim they are 'responding naturally' or being 'completely objective' do not know themselves" (p. 8). *Know* in this sense means understanding how the reading of a text is inevitably bound up with how one sees the world, and what "normalcy" consists of in a culture. Thus, finding means to critically analyze texts, contexts, and experiences is an important part of imagining alternative perspectives through literary avenues and a way to explore oneself, society, and the world. One method for doing this work in English classrooms is to draw on critical schools of thought to examine texts. Schools of thought can be introduced via lenses (Appleman, 2014), and students might apply the primary considerations of a theoretical position to a piece they are studying (for instance, applying theories of gender when examining advertisements). Theories provide the undergirding of lenses and may be introduced through key authors in the field, forming an intertextual response to a literary piece and/or the context in which a piece was created. Regardless of how theories are introduced (again, see the Resource box on p. 70 for further reading), what is most important is that these theories are presented and used as *tools*, rather than as another avenue for interpretation to be evaluated as "correct" or "incorrect." Students should be the ones to determine whether a specific lens has restorying potential. To that end, we suggest that assignments reflect this attitude and do not require extolling the virtues or describing the outcomes of applying a certain lens to a certain text; rather, students might be asked to describe the usefulness or appropriateness of different critical theoretical approaches. For example, rather than having students read about a particular critical approach (say, reading the work of Audre Lorde or Judith Butler in connection with gender constructs) and then apply the concept of gender critique to a preselected text, students might be asked to what extent such an approach is useful, valuable, or salient in a particular context, allowing them to assess the value of a given approach while becoming familiar with it. Similarly, rather than ask students to apply a gendered critique to an advertisement or short story they are examining, a teacher might ask students what the piece evokes for them, what the piece says about society or a group of people, and then follow up with questions and readings that build on students' natural critiques. These may diverge from the teacher's analysis (for instance, perhaps students critique classism and inequality, leading the teacher to recommend readings related to capitalism and Marxism), but they may lead students down a critical path that directly connects to their inductive observations.

- **Draw on critical lenses as a bridge to examining and acting on power imbalances in local contexts.** Who benefits from students studying critical stances in the English classroom? At first glance, it's clear that students do; theories help students find alternative ways of analyzing texts. Theories assist students in restorying narratives in ways that resist and complicate perspectives. So . . . what do students *do* with this knowledge, and where or how do they use it moving forward? How does valuing alternative perspectives translate into *acting to restore relationships and opening pathways of resistance* in the restorative justice classroom? We offer several ways:

○ Ensure that students continue to have opportunities to respond to texts in critical ways throughout the school year and in multiple capacities (i.e., not just during a critical views unit or in the context of a specific text). This might entail teacher and students bringing in other texts (including film and other nonprint materials) to gain a deeper appreciation or understanding of critical schools of thought. For instance, after studying a text that illustrates elements of a particular theory (perhaps students read Derrick Bell's work in order to gain an understanding of critical race theory [CRT]), students might be asked to bring in texts that they feel exemplify the theory in nuanced ways. (For instance, a student might bring in an online article discussing racial disparities in judicial sentencing practices to discuss in connection with Bell's work and CRT.)

○ As anyone who has immersed themselves in a critical perspective knows, once a veil has been drawn away, the world continues to open with possibilities. Critical perspectives lend themselves not just to the work of reading texts, but also to the work of living. Encourage students to apply their newfound critical lenses to contexts and settings they see every day, bringing in examples for the class to analyze (not just textual) and applying these lenses to everyday interactions, issues, and concerns. Be open to students directing their evaluation at the classroom and school, and model what it looks like to engage in critical discourse around the context you share with them. This may forge avenues for further reflection and restoration in the classroom community.

○ Bring students' growing critical perspectives to a place of critical action and resistance in the school, local community, and beyond. Help students think about criticality as connected to advocacy, and create multiple projects and opportunities that engage critical consciousness, literacy, and social change. Such a project might be located in the school (e.g., one student notices the school's chess club is composed only of boys), in the community (e.g., another student is disturbed by the disproportionate way young people of color are harassed and followed around when they walk into local stores), or in the world (see Connor's example in the following classroom vignette). Design projects (individual, small group, or whole class) that encourage students to put their deepening understanding of critical perspectives to work through literate means (writing letters, speeches, op-eds; organizing protests, etc.) and in ways that are personal, relevant, and civically minded (see Emilie's example in the vignette on pp. 67–69). Importantly, as part of this process, be sure to defer to students' expertise and desires; ask them what they want to do with the information they have, what possible solutions they imagine, and what tools they might already have at their disposal to engage in this work.

Into the Classroom: Fostering a Critical, Action-Oriented Consciousness

Connor Beaudoin, grades 6–9 English teacher

In my second year of teaching, I taught a combined grades 7–8 English class. Toward the end of the year, we read *A Long Walk to Water* by Linda Sue Park. This short novel follows the true story of Salva Dut, a Sudanese Lost Boy, mirrored by the story of the fictional character Nya, a young village girl, as they deal with personal strife and the extreme difficulties that accompany growing up in South Sudan. Through feats of absolute courage and bravery, both characters rise above life's obstacles to give back to the place they both call home. The drive behind using this book was to open my students' eyes to the different types of struggles individuals around the world must face. In addition to reading the text, we also read articles and did research on Sudan's history and the country's current state of affairs. As our wealth of knowledge about the country grew, my students began to understand the extreme daily struggle the Sudanese people face in finding water. Conversations about what we felt were our daily struggles began to put the seriousness that access to clean water possesses in perspective. At the end of a class period, after we had finished the book, I posed a simple question to my students: "Now what? What can we do?"

Through our research on the book, students had discovered that Salva Dut had started a nonprofit organization called Water for South Sudan. The organization works with villages across South Sudan to install wells that supply water to all of the surrounding villages. Without prompting, a student suggested that we could raise money and donate it to the organization. As this idea gained momentum with the class, another student chipped in that we could start a GoFundMe page. Having never heard of GoFundMe, I immediately Googled it and created an account right on the spot with the class. That night my students and I shared the link on our Facebook pages, and the donations began to pour in. Each day in class, we would track our progress (we set a goal of raising $300). I always made sure that checking our progress was a mini-celebration (a common refrain was "Drummmmmm rollllllll, please!"). Hearing the cheers and seeing the smiles on my students' faces taught me more about the importance of social activism than I could ever teach them. After only two weeks, my classes had raised more than $500 dollars. In addition to writing personalized thank-you notes to those who had donated, the students engaged in organic conversations on the power of social media and actionable steps we as individuals can take to create change, not only around the world, but also in our own backyards.

Into the Classroom: Fostering a Critical, Action-Oriented Consciousness

Emilie Homan, grade 12 English teacher

To me, my job as a teacher is not to sit on a plane of knowledge above my students, attempting to bring them to my level and prescribing ideas of what it means to be "educated." Rather, it means that I stand *under* my students, carrying them on my shoulders, supporting them, and pushing them upward toward their goals. In this classroom the students are inspired by, but not dependent on, me. One way I have enacted this student-centered philosophy of teaching is through a critically conscious project I have used every year since student teaching: the multigenre research project.

The multigenre research project, in which students research a topic of interest through multiple modalities and then decide how to address their issue, is one I have honed through the guidance of many other teachers and the experience of many different classes. In the past, I usually prescribed the steps students needed to take during the course of the project. However, in reflecting on my student-centered goals, this year the project relied entirely on the perspectives, goals, and problem-solving skills of the students. I gave them direction, but ultimately *their* curiosity would do the teaching. The goal of this project is for students to identify a social problem, nurture their literary and critical consciousness through examining and connecting multiple kinds of texts, and disseminate their findings as a form of critical action.

The project began by asking students about pressing social concerns they saw in the world: not a problem that *I* wanted solved, or a problem that I *assumed* they wanted solved. Through extensive scaffolding, community building, and discussion, students were tasked with recognizing a social issue or problem they held close to their hearts. This issue served as the primary question they would address through the multigenre research project. Once students identified a social issue they wanted to fix, solve, change, modify, or bring awareness to, they formed their own essential questions. Because students were given the freedom to ask questions they actually wanted answers to, their questions were reflective of what they genuinely wanted to learn. These questions included:

- "What is Islamophobia, why is it a global issue, and what strategies can the United States government use to resolve this global issue?"

- "Why is the Latin American Drug War a global issue, and how can the people involved solve this issue?"

- "How is agriculture affecting climate change, and how can global leaders make change to fix this problem?"

- "Why are Asians misrepresented in media, why is this misrepresentation an issue in the United States, and how can we bring awareness to this issue?"

After defining their questions, students began research with the goal of eventually answering their questions with evidence and through research. We talked about the importance of evaluating sources for credibility and usefulness. We explored bias, both subtle and obvious, and we discussed the tools that writers use to persuade their audience. After these discussions, I gave students the freedom to explore and use classroom resources each day as they saw fit. Because of the trust, flexibility, and confidence I gave students, they became immersed in their research. No source was off-limits, allowing students to access and reference materials they used in their everyday lives. Students were reading articles, bingeing on podcasts, interviewing people in the community, discussing Netflix documentaries. Within their research, students grasped the real logos and ethos of their topics, but I also wanted them to explore the pathos of their topics. Students also read fiction that helped them answer their essential question. They picked these novels based on synopsis and interest, and I encouraged them to put down books they weren't connecting with in favor of new ones. These reading experiences helped students see connections between various genres while enhancing the critiques the students were bringing to their essential questions. For example, one student, who studied the militarization of police and brutality toward African Americans and other people of color, chose to read *All American Boys* by Jason Reynolds and Brendan Kiely. Another student, who was studying mass incarceration in the United States, read *In Warm Blood: Prison and Privilege, Hurt and Heart* by local authors Judith Gwinn Adrian and DarRen Morris. The student was inspired to tackle this topic after we went to an art exhibit to see DarRen Morris's work and listened to Judith Adrian speak.

Once students collected research on their essential questions and read their novels, they moved on to the next step: creating and educating others. I asked students to create both a nonfiction and a fiction piece of writing that answered their essential question. As part of this assignment, students wrote in a genre of nonfiction that they had never explored before. This new exploration led them to create scripts for podcasts, magazine articles, brochures for the student services department, public service announcements, television advertisements, short stories, series of poems, graphic novels, and more—whatever genre best fit their topic and unique set of skills. However, in order to write in these various genres, students had to conduct a different kind of research. They had to learn about and adhere to genre guidelines. I provided some tools for accessing genres, but for any questions relating to the style, formality, formatting, or anything else specific to the genre, my motto became "You tell me"; I was interested in their observations, not in telling them what various genres consist of. When I stopped being an "answer vending machine" for students, they found their answers for themselves through inductively examining texts within these genres, and they interpreted these genre guidelines in new and innovative ways. Through these pieces of writing, I saw novel, critical, and creative ideas that I had never witnessed from students or even heard of before.

To build on this creativity, students also produced a visual piece that spoke to their essential question without using any words. To do this, students had to really explore alternative forms of communication. I was amazed at what these students came up with: they were cooking and baking, designing museums in Google SketchUp, creating social interactions and simulations in Sims (a life simulation game series), and choreographing contemporary and lyrical dance routines. Once again, by trusting my students, I gave them the space to learn and explore while also showcasing their unique talents and interests.

Eventually, each student took all of these pieces and designed a website to educate others about their social issue. Through this website, students were able to describe and reflect on the entire process of the multigenre research project. The website included not only their essential question, research reflections, thesis, nonfiction piece, fiction piece, and visual piece, but also reflections on each piece, including how they decided what to ask and how to format their reflections. Students wrote about how each genre and component of the project amplified their message for their audience. They chose which sources to use and how to use them, determined the answer to their essential question, and decided how to present and communicate this answer.

Finally, students shared their websites in a symposium to which they invited friends, family, previous teachers, and community members to learn about their work. Students used this opportunity to engage in critical action and spoke with authority and passion about their topics. The pride they felt in their work was palpable. And the consequences of this project have been notable. Now when students are presented with information that is concerning or upsetting, I hear them asking for clarity. I see that students are more critical of the sources put in front of them. I have seen a decline in students spreading information merely for excitement and a rise in students sharing facts with others because they are pertinent and true.

Because of this project, I have heard many students speak differently about the social issues that face our society today. For instance, prior to this project and throughout the year, I often heard kids spreading inaccurate information and news they had found on blogs and Reddit. The ultimate goal seemed to be to achieve the "gasp" effect rather than to dispense information that might be useful; this was especially prevalent after the presidential election. After the multigenre project unit, I overheard my students talking about their frustrations with current leadership. Rather than giving the responses I was used to ("No way!" or "Oh my god!"), I heard students responding with "Where did you get that information?" and "Who told you that? Where did they get their information?" This was especially exciting because they were asking these critical questions even about stories that affirmed their beliefs. I have also seen a shift in students' understanding of how they can impact others in their sphere of influence. Rather than speaking in hypotheticals and "shoulds" on behalf of society, the government, or people of authority, students are identifying and critiquing problems in a sophisticated manner and seeing themselves as part of the solution. One student reached out to a prison in Wisconsin and is now a pen pal with one of the incarcerated individuals. Another student decided to volunteer at Domestic Abuse Intervention Services (DAIS). One student is now hoping to study educational policy and has been listening to various NPR podcasts to learn about how education functions and affects people in the United States. I have two students who are now going to college with the hopes of studying law and working for the Innocence Project!

Conclusion

Writing about community and social engagement in restorative justice in education, Evans and Vaandering (2016) explain:

> The starting point in "how we are when we are together" is relationships rather than rules, people rather than policies, honoring capacity rather than evaluating ability, creating meaning rather than imposing knowledge, asking rather than telling, and well-being rather than merit-based success. This does not imply that rules, policies,

Resource Spotlight: Developing Critical, Actionable Consciousness with Students

Appleman, Deborah. *Critical Encounters in Secondary English: Teaching Literary Theory to Adolescents.* 3rd ed. New York: Teachers College Press, 2015.

Garcia, Antero. *Critical Foundations in Young Adult Literature: Challenging Genres.* Rotterdam, Netherlands: Sense Publishers, 2013.

Morrell, Ernest, Rudy Dueñas, Veronica Garcia, and Jorge López. *Critical Media Pedagogy: Teaching for Achievement in City Schools.* New York: Teachers College Press, 2013.

Rethinking Schools: http://www.rethinking schools.org/index.shtml.

Zemelman, Steven. *From Inquiry to Action: Civic Engagement with Project-Based Learning in All Content Areas.* Portsmouth, NH: Heinemann, 2016.

evaluation, telling, and success are irrelevant; it simply means that these serve the needs of people living within community, not the other way around. (p. 12)

Following this ethos in the ELA classroom means that teachers co-create space for the community—students and teacher together—to collaborate in meaning-making experiences that open new pathways for understanding, learning, and resistance. This approach puts communal exploration rather than compliance at the center, inviting in always-changing ways of being, seeing, and doing. Creating spaces that *restore, restory,* and *resist.*

As teachers journey toward establishing a restorative classroom space, we remind them that this process is not easy, unidirectional, or capable of being implemented overnight. The practices we recommend here are part of a broader shift in imagining the purpose of our classrooms—who they serve, who they are currently leaving at the door, and how we might invite all students in. They are not only practices, but also a framework for beginning the process of summoning a pedagogic community. In this same vein, we invite teachers on this journey toward fostering restorative justice English education spaces, using our curricular powers to get there.

Assessing Our Spaces and Ourselves

Why do we send children to school?

It is a deceptively simple question, one that has evoked impassioned rhetoric and divisive policies, driven research agendas and pedagogical methodologies. It has ultimately both conformed to and shaped the fabric of American society. Without a clear rejoinder, there is one optimistic answer that surfaces above others: opportunity. We send our children to school because we want them to have opportunities. To learn. To connect. To grow. To shape themselves, each other, and the world. Milner (2010) explains our desire for opportunity in terms of its vitality for success and its significant absence for many students in US schools, observing:

> Too many students in P–12 institutions have not been provided an opportunity to develop into successful students because our educational system has not been structurally designed to do so. Opportunity is at the core of success and failure in society as well as in schools. I believe a focus on an achievement gap places too much blame and emphasis on students themselves as individuals and not enough attention on why gaps and disparities are commonplace in schools across the country. (p. 8)

Milner finds that this rhetoric of the achievement gap positions students who do not fit the White-centric (and, we would add, heteronormative and ableist) perspective in education as ultimately deficient, and ignores the powerful strengths and expertise with which students enter classrooms. Drawing from Ladson-Billings (2006), he explains that the perceived "gap" obscures the real *education debt* that minoritized students are owed. This debt is, at its core, a debt of opportunity. But educational opportunities can be expanded, constructed, or altered by educators. English teachers, as marshals and conjurers of stories, have a profoundly important role in creating new narratives of success and opportunity through fashioning restorative, equitable, and just learning environments. It is the teacher's role in creating such environments that lies at the heart of this book.

How do we know if we are ready and able to create restorative spaces? The answer lies in a combination of assessing our spaces, our practices, and ourselves to determine areas for improvement, and formatively checking in on those spaces and students to determine next steps. In Chapter 2, we outlined some of the ways educators can prepare for restorative conversations and Circle processes with youth. In this chapter, then, we turn to ourselves, our pedagogy, and our classrooms, assessing how and if we are calling in students and perspectives. We address the following questions:

- How can teachers actively engage in self-assessment work?
- In what ways can teachers assess their classrooms to determine whether they are collaboratively and actively fostering inclusive, restorative spaces?
- In what ways can teachers engage in formative assessment to determine the efficacy of restorative justice practices in their classroom spaces?

To answer these questions, we address planning for personal development and classroom development as two distinct yet still profoundly interconnected components.

Personal Development: Auditing the Self

One thing we have found as practitioners, teachers, and teacher educators is that teachers are perennial, lifelong learners. English teachers in particular have a penchant for reading to learn about the world and themselves. For teachers on the path to becoming restorative leaders, the most important place to start is with the *self*, retraining our minds to be more critical of our own biases. It is through examining and altering our perspectives as adults that change in school spaces will occur; as Rita reminds us, "We [adults] are the ones who made this mess, and now we have to fix this!"

An important assessment step toward fostering a restorative classroom is teacher self-assessment and the resulting creation of a personal learning development plan, engaging in a process of *auditing the self*. We firmly believe that critically examining ourselves for potential areas of growth in our work with others leads to the surfacing of possible—perhaps even previously unseen—biases, which leads to new understandings of history, others, and the self, ultimately opening pathways to further learning opportunities. Use the steps outlined in the following sections as a starting point to begin thinking, reflecting on, and planning your personal development toward the creation of a restorative classroom space.

Step 1. Consider Areas of Growth

There is not one answer to the question of where and how each of us needs to grow. Growth in this context not only refers to our own interests, but also encompasses areas and identities that we may not know much about and, as instructors of young people, need to become more knowledgeable about. Where to begin?

One way may be to reflect on your teaching environment and what you might/could/should know more about in relation to your students, classroom, and community. Perhaps you teach in a classroom with a wealth of recently arrived immigrant students and/or parents and you want to learn more about how the history of immigration intersects with schooling and education in the United States. Perhaps you teach in a school where African American students are being disproportionately suspended or expelled and you want to understand how and why this might be the case, learn the history of the school-to-prison pipeline, and consider how you might (perhaps unintentionally) be contributing to this system. Perhaps you teach in a mainly White classroom space and you want to learn more about your own biases in some specific way to ensure you are not communicating destructive ideas to your students. Perhaps you have heard recently about the importance of creating safe spaces for genderqueer and nonbinary students and you wish to understand in more depth the concept of "safe space" with regard to gender identity. Think about areas in which you might need to grow or become more knowledgeable about regarding identities, culture, and experience.[12]

Take a moment to jot down as many of these areas for growth as you can. You might want to use a chart like this:

Concern	Why I am concerned	Questions I have about this area

Step 2. Locate Resources: Understanding Context, Impact, and History

Once you have your list, hone in on a specific area or multiple areas you wish to immediately look into (depending on how much reading time you have!). Here you begin your research and reading process. For instance, you may have jotted down "How can safe spaces be created for all students in diverse classrooms?" as a question, and thus something you want to learn more about. Now you begin looking for material to help you understand this concept in more depth and create a syllabus of learning material for yourself. Some potential starting points:

- Chapter 1 of this book
- Friends, colleagues, and students who might have recommendations
- Open-source academic journals and articles ("Open source" simply means that you don't need to pay or have special permissions—such as belonging to a college or university community—to have access to materials. A Google search will reveal many journals and sites dedicated to culling articles that don't require payment for materials.)
- Online book and video retailers (where a quick keyword search often yields multiple results and suggestions)
- Social media (Organizations like Teachers for Social Justice, among many others, have Facebook or Twitter groups where members can write posts asking for reading recommendations.)
- News outlets (The *New York Times*, *Huffington Post*, and other publications devote entire sites to discussing various issues in the field of education and classroom pedagogy.)
- Experts in the field (One way to begin this process is by using keywords and a search engine, such as Google Scholar. Once you have a list of publications you are interested in by a specific individual, you might want to check out their books from a local library, buy a version online, or find their articles through open-source journals. Google Scholar itself usually indicates when specific articles or books are available for free download online.)
- YouTube and other open-source video sites (There are thousands of videos on multiple phenomena and the histories of various subjects. Because anyone can post on these sites, however, be sure to enter such portals with a critical eye.)

As you build and expand your reading list, be sure to historicize your search; as we discussed in Chapter 1, gaining an understanding of historical context is essential to understanding how and why movements, mindsets, and society exist as they do. Try to include material that fosters a historical understanding of current conditions in order to develop a sociocritical literacy (Gutiérrez, 2008a, 2008b).

Step 3. Reflect and Take Action

As you engage in your personalized syllabus, keep a journal of your thoughts, wonderings, and particularly salient quotes. Throughout your research, take time to pause and reflect on the new information you are finding, what this learning is making you think about, and what you might want to do based on the information. One way to do this is by responding to the following questions as you read:

- Am I opening myself up to alternative stances on [chosen area]?
- How is what I am learning shifting my initial view of [chosen area]?
- How does understanding the history surrounding [chosen area] alter or expand my understanding of this topic/the world/society?
- How do I see what I am learning playing out in society? In my school? Among my colleagues? Among my students? In my classroom?
- What can and do I want to change based on what I am learning?

Inevitably, as you engage with your list, some material will become more topical or influential than others. Some material will encourage you to explore different or further avenues of study. Be open to changing, developing, and altering your learning goals as particular subjects arise in your reading, in your classroom, and in your life. For instance, as you read, consider how you are a mediator of messages in your classroom. Are there particular ways you emit or transfer messages through your curriculum? How might you change your texts, unit plans, or curriculum to be more inclusive or critical? Perhaps a holiday or particular reading month (e.g., Black History Month, Thanksgiving) is coming up. Use this opportunity to read more about the histories and experiences of these celebrations, incorporating your newfound knowledge into your classroom through choice of texts, writing prompts, and presentation of material. We explore further conduits for change in the later section on classroom development.

Reading into the First Year: Building My Syllabus

Julie Kesti, middle school ELA teacher

I am eight months into my first year of teaching. It feels great to say that. Finishing a master's degree gave me a sense of accomplishment, but realizing that I will indeed make it to the end of my first year of teaching is a thrill, a deep sigh, a feeling of exhaustion, and an awareness that every cell of my body has been stretched and challenged over the last eight months. The success of each class period has been so deeply connected to keeping my breath and awareness slow and steady, carefully considering as many decisions as possible along the way.

During my graduate program, I made good use of the university library and maintained evolving piles of books on the floor of my student apartment. I "read" audiobooks on my four-hour drives home on the weekends and listened to podcasts as I hiked through the woods along the lake. I pledged to continue this side hustle of exploration once my teaching career was underway in another state. There was a drop-off in activity in the first weeks of school, when I'd come home, collapse on the living room floor, and cry from exhaustion, but inevitably I'd find a scrap of a note I'd jotted down during my graduate program and be reminded to keep fueling myself beyond the day-to-day demands of teaching. Such fueling entailed reading. Reading to inspire, challenge, and lend nuance to my thinking and practice. Some of this includes looking for inspiration in teacher books by people such as Janet Allen and Pernille Ripp, but this reading is not just about classroom strategy. This is reading that parallels my purpose for being in the classroom, which is to remember that human beings are endlessly complex and interesting, and that understanding the world is a process that goes on and on, and that being literate is powerful. This extracurricular reading is for my own delight and expansion, but it is also about walking a way of life that I hope will transfer to my students and help them figure out how they best explore and navigate the world.

Much of my reading my first year has been an attempt to understand my position in society and how that relates to and diverges from that of my students. In my school, most of the staff are White, myself included, but I do not have a single White student in my classes. Over half of our students are refugees from minority groups from Burma, Laos, and other parts of Southeast Asia. The two other biggest groups in the school are Black (African American and African) and Latinx students. It's a wonderful mix of people and stories.

Over the course of this school year, I've realized that when I am almost anywhere else other than school there are . . . so many White people. Everywhere. I lived in China before graduate school, and I think my feeling now reflects that experience somewhat: White faces were usually the exception in China, and hearing my own language was also uncommon. But in this case, I am not in another country; I'm not even driving in from the suburbs. I'm commuting from another part of the city. This viscerally drives home for me how segregated the city I teach in is and how White my own personal world is. I knew this before, but I know it in a different way now, in a way that I can't easily push to a corner of my mind. It is an uncomfortable fact, an embarrassing and sometimes painful fact. I don't state this simply to lament it or to humbly express White guilt, but because I understand that I need to keep these families, these disparities, these divisions clear in my mind and try to understand them so that I am not creating a classroom world that is just a mirror of the segregated life of the Twin Cities. I want the space to reflect something better, wider, more interesting: something that validates, celebrates, enjoys, and envisions a breadth of experiences.

I don't expect to have this sorted out by a specific date, or maybe ever. It requires a multifaceted approach to reflecting, reading, and acting on what I learn. Early this year, as I became aware of my continuing need to think deeply about my Whiteness, context, and pedagogy, I read *For White Folks Who Teach in the Hood . . . and the Rest of Y'all Too: Reality Pedagogy and Urban Education* by Christopher Emdin, who stresses the importance of creating spaces and ways for students to help create the classroom. My small beginnings at this have included a student wall where they can write and draw whatever they want, as well as having students introduce the day's learning and summarize it at the end of class. Emdin's book also advises me to be on the lookout for the ways in which I may be misreading or just plain ignorant of what and how my students might be trying to communicate, or even simply their ways of being in the world.

I have dedicated this year to becoming aware of how my positionality and cultural background affect how I may (mis)read students and, as part of this endeavor, learning as much as possible about students' backgrounds, interests, and everyday lives. Building this awareness is earnest and serious, but it's also exciting and fun, and has guided the multigenre texts I have chosen to explore as part of my personal development—in other words, my personal syllabus. I was able to attend a reading by some of the contributors to Sun Yung Shin's *A Good Time for the Truth: Race in Minnesota* in the fall. The writers' words pushed against all the entrenched ideas people have about being "Minnesotan"—being nice, politely passive, Scandinavian, and probably White. The authors shared very clear incidents of racism they have faced in Minnesota that I think most White people would be clueless (and defensive) about. These are the stories that are hard to discuss but that are essential to revealing the ways that privilege works.

I also learn a lot from my students directly. I gain more functional literacy in K-pop and hip-hop by viewing videos and listening to music my students recommend to me, and I figure out things like the reasons why some kids get a haircut and then cover it with a hoodie for two weeks by reading YA books like *The Hate U Give* by Angie Thomas. I piece together key fears and foods as my students tell me about Facebook rumors such as clown scares and threats of Trumpian price hikes on Little Debbie Honey Buns, heading to my computer and looking these up after teaching hours. I listen intently and ask my students questions while sharing stories and pieces of my life, building relationships as I come to understand their hopes, concerns, lives, ideas, and experiences as they move through the world.

To help me consider my positionality as a White woman, I explore a variety of media, just as I share a variety of media with my students. I follow @swellvalleybloodpulse on Instagram, a young feminist academic who regularly pushes my thinking, reminding me not to take any aspect of gender for granted and prompting me to help my students think about gender as well. I listen to NPR's *Code Switch* podcast and Phoebe Robinson's *Sooo Many White Guys* podcast to learn from diverse artists, writers, and leaders and to keep pushing back in my brain the narratives of White dominance that have been fed to me my whole life. Both of these podcasts are hosted by people of color who speak vividly on how Whiteness is always centered—listening to their perspectives helps me see outside my perspective in ways that go beyond just a theoretical understanding. Movies and documentaries are some of my favorite points of departure, and this year has provided Ava DuVernay's *13th*, Barry Jenkins's *Moonlight*, and Raoul Peck's *I Am Not Your Negro*. I made it to the theater for the musical *Fun Home* and saw how powerfully a youth narrative about identity and sexuality can move an audience. It becomes an adventure of discovery as one source leads to another—I hear an ad for one podcast on another, jot down a name from the Sunday newspaper, hear from my union about a film showing, or, in the case of Alison Bechdel's *Fun Home*, have a book recommended to me in line at a coffee shop. I sometimes feel like half the emails in my personal inbox are from myself because I send myself notes on leads to follow up on. The *13th* screening was particularly powerful because it was a showing for educators, but a handful of students were there. Several of the students were extremely angry after the showing, feeling vulnerable because they'd watched the screening in a room with many White people. Their voicing their anger helped me understand that even as I want to be with my students in conversations about race, my Whiteness alone may make that discussion feel less safe, no matter how much I try to understand. This makes me careful about taking on an authoritative role when talking about race in the classroom. It reinforces my own ignorance and need to keep listening and learning, working to open the space for my students to act as guides, while also not forcing them into a spotlight if they aren't ready or comfortable.

I watched the series *13 Reasons Why*—the Netflix show based on Jay Asher's book—because all of my students were watching it or reading the book. At first I thought, "Oh, these adults are such caricatures!" but then I took to heart that adults probably very often look like caricatures to 12-year-olds. Part of why the story resonates so strongly is that it shows the distance between what adults understand of kids' worlds and what kids really experience. With my students I read Thanhha Lai's *Inside Out and Back Again*, an immigrant story told in verse. The narrative of fleeing a war is one that half of my students related to personally and that other students and I could empathize with and learn from, while also easily relating to the parts about starting a new school, feeling different, and trying to figure out a new place. I ordered *The Hate U Give* by Angie Thomas for my students but snuck it off the shelf and read it first. It showed me how overly simple my understanding of Jordan athletic shoes is. It reminded me that there are other versions of the happy birthday song, that some kids don't go outside after school, and that stereotype threat is felt in so many moments for so many children, particularly for students of color in White school environments.

The world I grew up in was so, so White and so defined by the limited ideals promoted by mainstream popular culture and the literary canon. Although progress has been made in the last two decades and my students are not growing up completely in that world, our popular culture and canon still have a long way to go to richly reflect their lives. This truth affirms my commitment to ensuring that literature and communication are not presented as the work of wealthy White people in other places. That's not an accurate telling of what the world is made of. This commitment means that I offer many and varied opportunities for my students to share their experiences of the world, and that I value this work by responding to it, posting it, and helping them share it with each other. It means that we work with a variety of texts in class—from the popular to the more "serious"—just like the texts that make up my syllabus. Many of my students feel that school is a very different place from the rest of their lives, run by adults who don't look or talk like most of the adults in their lives, and who may not know how it feels to be them and traverse the city. Other students' memories are of places they may never return to, or their family stories are set in places they have never been. We may all feel far from home, we may feel out of place, but as a teacher it is my hope and ultimate goal to create a new space together.

Julie's Personal Syllabus

Quarter 1 Reading

A Seat at the Table (album) by Solange
Black Messiah (album) by D'Angelo and the Vanguard

The Crossover (book) by Kwame Alexander

Passing (book) by Nella Larsen

Daughters of the Dust (film) by Julie Dash

Code Switch (podcast) by NPR

For White Folks Who Teach in the Hood . . . and the Rest of Y'all Too (book) by Christopher Emdin

Yellow Brick Roads (book) by Janet Allen

Quarter 2 Reading

Inside Out and Back Again (book) by Thanhha Lai

Losing Ground (film) by Kathleen Collins

"We Got It from Here—Thank You 4 Your Service" (2017 SXSWedu keynote) by Christopher Emdin

We Got It from Here—Thank You 4 Your Service (album) by A Tribe Called Quest

13 Reasons Why (Netflix series)

@swellvalleybloodpulse (Instagram feed)

Quarter 3 Reading

Moonlight (film) by Barry Jenkins

The Tiger Rising (book) by Kate DiCamillo

The Rookie Podcast by Tavi Gevinson

The Bridge Called My Back (book) edited by Cherríe Moraga and Gloria Anzaldúa

Marbles: Mania, Depression, Michelangelo, and Me (graphic memoir) by Ellen Forney

Teen Vogue (magazine)

Grace and the Fever (book) by Zan Romanoff

The Hate U Give (book) by Angie Thomas

I Am Not Your Negro (film) by Raoul Peck

Quarter 4 Reading

DAMN. (album) by Kendrick Lamar

Can't Stop Won't Stop: A History of the Hip-Hop Generation (book) by Jeff Chang

So Many White Guys (podcast) by Phoebe Robinson

Punished by Rewards (book) by Alfie Kohn

A Good Time for the Truth: Race in Minnesota (book) edited by Sun Yung Shin

Passionate Learners (book) by Pernille Ripp

Culture and Power in the Classroom (book) by Antonia Darder

Fun Home (book and musical) by Alison Bechdel

Poetry off the Shelf (podcast) by the Poetry Foundation

13th (film) by Ava DuVernay

Classroom Development: Examining Learning Contexts

As we mentioned at the outset of this book, there is no "magic formula" or complete list of best practices for the creation of a restorative classroom space. Mindset, stance, and an unrelenting desire to respond to *all* student needs are the cornerstone of a classroom dedicated to building community and restoring peace and well-being. However, with this in mind, we articulate a number of suggested practices that lead to classrooms where equity, empowerment, and flexibility are prioritized (see also Chapter 3); these classrooms open up space for all voices to be heard (vocally and metaphorically), for all student contributions to be elicited and valued, for texts to reflect "windows and mirrors" and the curriculum to integrate students' lives, and for criticality to be an actionable constituent of the learning space.

Student Survey

Student surveys can be used in multiple ways throughout the year to understand how your students are feeling in your classroom, giving you insight into whether students perceive that their voices are being encouraged and valued, and to what extent students feel your class is a place where their well-being is maintained and promoted. Responses to the following survey can be an excellent starting point for examining possible areas for change in your classroom. Continued survey-type check-ins (using or extending the following questions) that focus on affective responses to classroom processes can provide deep, continuous insight into the extent to which your classroom is a space where students know that their thoughts and ideas are appreciated.

Note: This survey can be optional and/or anonymous, based on the candidness of the responses you expect or wish to receive. You may also want to make this an online survey (via Google Forms, SurveyMonkey, or another survey instrument), as this may make it easier to compile and examine responses.

Name (Optional)_____

Student Survey: Our Class

1. How do you feel in this class most of the time?
2. Do you feel safe (emotionally, physically, and in other ways) in this class? Please help me understand why or why not.

---

3. Do you feel like the teacher in this class values your thoughts and ideas?
4. Do you feel like your thoughts and ideas are valued in this class by other students?
5. Do you feel that the teacher values all thoughts and ideas presented in this class, regardless of who says them or where they come from?
6. Do you feel that you have the opportunity to voice your opinion (either through speaking aloud, writing, or in another form) in this class?
7. Do you feel that all students are given the opportunity to speak (either through speaking aloud, writing, or in another form) in this class?
8. Do you often have the chance to hear what your fellow students think in this class?
9. What else do you think I should know about what it is like to be in this class?
10. Is there anything that would make this class a better experience for you?

Who Speaks and Who Is Valued? An Observation Exercise

Do you have a sense of how dialogue functions in your classroom and whose viewpoints are valued in the process of learning? One helpful way to assess the extent to which voices are elicited and capitalized on is through observing classroom dialogue patterns and assessing what they mean for and about your community. Consider dialogue and dialogue patterns by engaging in the following exercise throughout the year:

Who Speaks and Who Is Valued?

- Prepare to videotape, audio-record, or closely observe your classroom. Videotaping is ideal, as it allows you to observe body language in addition to verbal discourse, but that may not be possible depending on availability of technology or school policy. If you plan on videotaping, be sure to check with your administration to ensure that this process is allowed in your classroom.

- Review your recording (or notes), paying attention to these questions:
  - Who spoke during class?
  - Who didn't speak?
  - How are contributions met in this class? (For instance, are contributions generally viewed as an invitation to explore new perspectives? Are they seen as a means to access a prespecified interpretation?)

- Do contributions invite new people to speak up, and if so, when?

- What patterns are you noticing?

- Do you suspect this is a typical day in terms of patterns you've noticed? Why or why not?

• Create a plan for addressing any patterns you've noticed through observing the class. This may involve further investigation. For instance, if you noticed that the same students voice their opinion each time the class is asked a question, what are some possible reasons for this response, and how can you disrupt this pattern? If you aren't sure, following up with further videotaping, looking at the video in conjunction with the Student Survey: Our Class, or checking in one on one with particular students about how they prefer to contribute may be a next step. You can also watch the video with your students to critically analyze communication patterns and collaboratively identify solutions that will disrupt problematic patterns; this activity itself is a relationship-building enterprise that promotes student voice, dialogue, and criticality.

Auditing Classroom Texts and the Integration of Lived Experiences

As we pointed out in Chapter 3, part of creating a classroom space where multiple perspectives are demonstrably valued consists of incorporating a diverse array of texts that reflect a "windows and mirrors" approach, in which students consistently see themselves and others represented classroom readings and activities. On your own or, ideally, in collaboration with your students, use the following questions to guide an audit of your classroom texts. Be sure to include independent reading books as well as those texts curated as part of the curriculum and Read Write Think Circle processes discussed in more depth in Chapter 5.

(Beginning) Questions for Auditing Classroom Texts

• To what extent are multiple perspectives represented in classroom texts?

• What perspectives are mostly represented? Which authors?

• What kinds of characters are predominantly represented?

• Are characters and perspectives represented fully or partially? Reductively or holistically?

• Are there any texts with problematic or harmful depictions of particular individuals or groups of people?

• What other patterns of difference or similarity (in perspective, authorial source, plot, characters) are you noticing across texts?

Into the Classroom: Augmenting Classroom Texts

Connor Beaudoin, grades 6–9 English teacher

When I first entered my combined fifth-sixth-grade ELA classroom as a first-year teacher, I quickly noticed that my school did not have an actual library on campus. Instead, there were miniature classroom libraries primarily found in ELA classrooms. In my room were three to four bookshelves that served as the middle school "library." The books had been acquired throughout the years before my arrival and ranged from Diary of Wimpy Kid books and *Cirque Du Freak* to the Divergent and Twilight series. There simply wasn't a variety in genre, author ethnicity, gender experience, or current young adult literature (YAL). I also found that many of the students who had been in the middle school for multiple years had read through all of the books that interested them. During my second year, our school started an initiative called "Stock the Shelves" to collect a larger breadth of books across the institution. The English department was in charge of selecting the books we wanted donors and members of the community to donate toward.

Not being completely up-to-date with which books were popular in the YAL community, I went to the University of Wisconsin's Cooperative Children's Book Center (CCBC) online list of top YAL books for that year. The list provided short descriptions on each book. I made sure to add books to our online catalog from authors of various backgrounds and locations, books that varied in gender expression, and books that represented multiculturalism. Donors and members of the community could donate money to a fund or personally buy a book from our list. We held a Stock the Shelves night for members of the community and raised more than $5,000. This money all went to purchasing new books for the classroom libraries in both the middle school and the high school. What I noticed, confirmed by other ELA teachers, was an immediate uptick in independent reading. We highlighted certain books and gave a quick synopsis at the start of classes, and students immediately wanted to get their hands on that book.

In addition to integrating diverse texts, we contend that incorporating materials from students' lives is essential to creating a curriculum fundamentally centered on student concerns and positioned as deeply relevant to student experiences. Review your curriculum to see if you are in fact creating consistent opportunities for student-centered learning, asking yourself the following questions:

- When I plan my units, am I generating activities, assignments, and assessment options that ask students to draw from their lived experiences? Where and how?

- Am I purposely building in questions to *every lesson* that encourages students to relate classroom learning and materials to their lives? Where and how?

- Am I valuing spontaneous student responses that connect individual experiences to the topic/subject/text at hand?

Acting to Restore: Criticality in Action

Creating pathways of resistance is a critical component of restorative justice work, as is restoring environments in which damage has been done. One way to assess how well you are focusing on criticality is to consider the continuum in Figure 4.1; ask yourself where your classroom falls on the continuum. To what extent are students using critical approaches or lenses and applying them in varied, action-oriented ways? Use Figure 4.1 as an initial investigative tool to reflect on current and future opportunities for critical work in your classroom and curriculum. It's important to note, however, that this chart is not symbolic of a linear trajectory within critical approaches. Various critical approaches and methodologies are important and necessary at different points; use this as a tool to think about how you are incorporating multiple forms of criticality into your classroom space.

Figure 4.1. Continuum of restorative justice.

Critical Instances ⟷			Actionable Responses
Students analyze something specific (an event, text, etc.) with a critical approach.	Students analyze events, texts, etc. across time using varied critical approaches.	Students utilize multiple critical approaches to identify unjust happenings in their context.	Students create a plan and execute an actionable response to an issue they have identified using critical approaches.

Into the Classroom: Critical Approaches across Units

Carla Oppenheimer, grade 10 English teacher

My goals in the classroom are to teach my students every day and across the year to practice empathy while taking a critical approach to the world around them. This year I launched my second semester with a study of commercials. Students loved playing detectives to find the hidden (or not-so-hidden) social messages embedded in advertisements. After watching and discussing several real commercials, I asked students to create and act out their own commercials that pushed back on a stereotype. To do this work, they needed to first analyze existing texts using critical approaches, and then use those critical approaches to identify injustices (in the form of stereotypes) they saw in their own lives. Examples included a commercial for dog food demonstrating that pit bulls are not dangerous, a commercial for sneakers that featured racially diverse basketball players, and an advertisement for a video game showing that girls can be just as passionate and skilled at playing video games as boys. This commercials activity promoted classroom community and gave students opportunities for movement, laughter, and joy in the classroom, even as they tackled heavy subject matter and complex rhetorical techniques.

In my classroom, however, we don't engage in critical experiences only when examining particular kinds of texts. Since early in the year, I have highlighted with my students the importance of approaching information critically. Toward the beginning of the year, we evaluated political websites for bias and accuracy in the weeks leading up to the election. As we began studying *Othello*, my students analyzed Iago's motives by considering social class, racism, and misogyny—all critical approaches that pushed them to examine multiple perspectives. The play also provided a centuries-old example of what happens when people act on bad information without critically examining its source, something my students noticed and I encouraged discussion around.

As a teacher, however, I also realize that criticality must be actionable. As the course progressed this year, I wanted to ensure that students had the opportunity to act on the critical perspectives we were incorporating. Midway through the year, I asked students to read about the potential impact of fake news on the election and write about who they thought was responsible. In our conversations and their writing, I helped students grapple with the concept of collective versus individual responsibility in a way that primed them to move their critical exploration into more purposeful explorations of social justice issues through research, our next unit. I collaborated with the school librarian to provide high-quality books and databases to support students' exploration and research, and I required student projects that both investigated a social justice issue and recommended at least one action step toward solving the problem. I used the term *action step* rather than *solution* to encourage students to think more concretely about what individuals and organizations can be doing.

One of the most interesting outcomes arose when two students chose the same issue—unintentional pregnancies—but came to completely different conclusions about the appropriate action steps. One student centered her research on abortion access in countries around the world and its positive effect on maternal health. Another student, whose cultural and religious beliefs did not support legal abortion, argued that the onus falls on educators and healthcare providers to provide more comprehensive sex education and birth control to young people. The two students presented their findings in the same class period, demonstrating that our classroom community could support multiple viewpoints on the same issue, so long as both were based in research. While at first glance this may not sound like an activity that approached "an actionable response to an issue," for many students this was their first effort to develop and communicate an informed opinion about a social justice issue. Knowing how to find out what action steps are possible is a crucial foundational skill that students will need in order to plan and execute further kinds of actionable responses in the future.

Conclusion

The work of creating and holding space dedicated to restorative justice is a process of, as Zehr (2002) reminds us, "putting right." Putting right in this sense does not mean putting back (as things were), but rather exploring the needs of a community, causes of harm, and possibilities for change. In the restorative justice English education classroom, this means reflecting on areas for personal and communal growth and co-creation. By looking inward, outward, and around us, we can begin assessing our current state of affairs and possibilities for change, partaking in the lifelong process of reflecting and changing.

Transforming Writing Instruction: Where Do We Go from Here?

As we completed this book, the United States elected Donald Trump as its forty-fifth president. Mr. Trump campaigned on a platform that promised to build a wall between the United States and Mexico and create a registry for Muslims. On the campaign trail, Mr. Trump mimicked a journalist with a disability, kept referring to African Americans as "the Blacks," and framed Mexicans as "rapists." Many of the comments and behaviors the country heard and witnessed would have been considered harmful, defiant, and punishable in many classrooms and schools. The night of the election, political commentator Van Jones graciously congratulated Trump, stating that he was raised to acknowledge people who achieve the unthinkable, before posing the question, "How do I explain this to my children?"

> It's hard to be a parent tonight for a lot of us. . . . You tell your kids, "Don't be a bully." You tell your kids, "Don't be a bigot." You tell your kids, "Do your homework and be prepared." And then you have this outcome. (November 8, 2016)

We are not here to debate the election results. We simply know as teachers, restorative justice practitioners, and educational researchers that our work moving forward may be even more challenging than before. We—like you—have asked ourselves the same question that Dr. Martin Luther King Jr. (2010) asked in what would become his final writings: *Where do we go from here?* We argue that restorative justice practices are a great place to begin. A restorative justice English education is not neutral, as we have explored in previous chapters, but rather provides opportunities to engage in difficult dialogues that explore race, class, gender, privilege, and so many topics that can be challenging, not just among colleagues and students but for families and loved ones as well. The day after the election, classroom teachers and RJ practitioners got to work. Minnesota School Safety Center Restorative Practices Specialist Nancy Riestenberg released a "Dear Colleague" letter encouraging educators to use the Circle process to "help students talk about their thoughts and feelings regarding the election." Reistenberg (November 9, 2016) suggested that teachers "use the full Circle process proactively" by following this protocol:

- Mindful silence, opening quote, song, story, or activity
- Meeting, getting acquainted round
- Common agreement round ("Which common agreement is important to you today?")
- Storytelling ("What value is important to you today, and who taught that value to you?")
- Addressing issues ("What are your thoughts about the election? Do you have questions about the process? What do you feel about the outcome?")
- Making a plan ("We all have different feelings and thoughts and hopes. What is one thing you can do to help others get along and learn?")
- Closing round, final quote, song, or activity

Similarly, on November 9, 2016, the Umoja Student Development Corporation posted a resource sheet on "Election Process Community Circles." Both Riestenberg and the Umoja Student Development Corporation encouraged participants to include writing as part of the Circle process. For example, Umoja suggested posing the question *How do we want to move forward as a class?* with examples such as writing letters to parents, family members, public figures, and even the presidential candidates themselves. Riestenberg suggested giving students and staff opportunities "to write what they are grateful for and to identify acts of kindness they can do each day." Teaching Tolerance published a blog post titled "The Day After" that recommended a journaling activity to "create space for reflection" (Mascareñaz, 2016).

We found this blog post to be a compelling reminder that the RJ English classroom must be prepared in advance to deal with potentially pressing issues.

This work begins on the first day of class. For example, Mascareñaz (2016) offers seven practices:

1. Begin within.
2. Get back to instruction.
3. Strengthen your classroom community.
4. Create space for reflection.
5. Discuss what respect means.
6. Look and plan ahead.
7. Talk about losing with grace.

What do these practices mean for English teachers? *Beginning within* simply means taking time to think about your own feelings and imagining how you might respond in ways that invite all students and all perspectives into the classroom. While *getting back to instruction* may sound like "business as usual," it's more of an acknowledgment to students and families that it's imperative that students continue to engage and be engaged in their learning. Learning is their right, as we've shown throughout this book, and instruction doesn't stop in Circles—Circles are one of many tools for instruction when you have a restorative justice culture. Getting back to instruction is our commitment to our students that communicates to them that they deserve to be engaged in high-quality work with rigor and purpose every day. *Strengthening classroom communities* signals the ongoing nature of a restorative justice approach. Facilitating a Circle the first week of school is not enough. Relationships need maintenance and sustenance, and it's important to check in with students through writing, partner sharing, and bringing some of this reflection into the Circle. We would argue that when we consider the importance of strengthening a classroom community, implementing restorative justice Circles early and often is ideal; thus, when there is an urgent issue or challenging moment, we aren't introducing Circles for the first time. Mascareñaz (2016), in describing *creating a space for reflection,* suggests journaling as an activity to give both students and teachers time and opportunity to share their ideas.

Mascareñaz's (2016) next suggestion of *discussing the meaning of respect* is also timely. We find that the word *respect* is used a lot in restorative justice Circles, and we often have to spend time in the process defining what respect means to various people; the sooner and more often your classroom can begin having these conversations, the less time defining the term itself will take when you're engaged in critical Circle processes. Many RJ educators will tell you that when they ask students how they define *respect,* the answers usually vary. Respect cannot be taken for granted and must be unpacked with the community.

Looking and planning ahead is more likely if you have prioritized getting "back to instruction" and "strengthening your classroom community," because then you are creating a future-oriented culture in which students understand that they have more than just the moment in front of them. In a future-oriented restorative classroom, students are positioned as agentive and capable of crafting a purposeful life. We would argue that it is the responsibility of restorative justice teachers—especially English teachers—to demonstrate how literacy can be used to make plans, look forward to next steps, and feel confident in our futures. Looking and planning ahead become a part of the class routine within a restorative justice paradigm. Note that we said "class routine." Yes, students can be a part of imagining the future direction of the work in class so they understand that everything they are doing is part of a larger arc that requires everyone's participation and contribution.

The final practice—*losing with grace*—is one that most adults have yet to master. Nevertheless, we have to teach winning with grace to our students, acknowledging that all of us—teachers, colleagues, students, families—have a range of beliefs and sociopolitical views. We believe it's important to ask a classroom community to consider collective "wins" and "losses" through questions such as "What do we all have to lose when [fill in the blank]?" or "What might we all stand to gain if we [fill in the blank]?"

As we consider these seven practices, we want to underscore how important it is to check in with yourself. Our days move so quickly in the classroom that we seldom have time to think about how we are feeling and what we are bringing into the classroom, so we must recognize the critical importance of self-care and self-awareness. Reflection can also take the form of imagining multiple perspectives, or what Appleman (2015) refers to as critical lenses, and through writing from different points of view. As difficult as it is during times of tumult to imagine what someone else is thinking or feeling, what the 2016 presidential election has taught all of us is not to assume we are on the same page or having the same experience(s) as others.

An Opportunity

Practicing justice in ELA classrooms is an opportunity to listen. When we listen to each other, we create the capacity to build schemas for understanding that people are more than monolithic images, stereotypes, or caricatures. Why do we default to these "cultural logos" of each other? Because they are easy, simplistic, and do not require that we spend time getting to know one another. However, if we do not take time early and often to listen, we all suffer later through a multitude of misunderstandings and misinterpretations of intention and impact. While some educators we work with are feeling defeated at this time, we see this moment as an opportunity to support teachers in embedding restorative justice and transformative justice into their practice. Here, we delineate between restorative and transformative. In the 25th anniversary edition of *Changing Lenses: Restorative Justice for Our Times*—the groundbreaking book offering a theoretical framework for restorative justice—Zehr (2015) cautions us about using "*re-* words." In the case of restorative justice, for example, Zehr posits that "many stakeholders and others interested in this field are not seeking to go back to a previous state of being but forward to new and better conditions" (p. 240). Thus, *transformative justice*, rather than restorative justice, invokes the need for change that makes a difference. Imagine the following scenarios:

- Week 1: On the first day of class, all seats are arranged in a circle. Students have time to engage in a freewrite responding to the questions "Who are you? Why are you here?" After students AND the teacher have time to write, the teacher/facilitator introduces a talking piece to signal that the person holding it is the only person talking, while everyone else has the gift of listening. The teacher discusses the role of restorative Circles and when students can expect to meet in Circles (we suggest at LEAST one consistent day a week if you have a forty-five- to fifty-minute block and twice if you have ninety-minute blocks two to three days a week).

- Week 2: In Circle, students AND the teacher write a maximum of four values they need in order to feel welcome in a community and describe these values (or offer examples). After students and the teacher have time to write down and describe values, they highlight one value to share with the group. If more than one student or the teacher chooses the same word/value, they spend time discussing the meaning. These shared values will become living documents that can be used to write parables, fables, short stories, and children's literature.

- Week 3: Teachers and students establish Read Write Think Circles (see the next section) using short readings such as op-eds, book excerpts, articles, poems, short stories, and so forth that are related to the reading and writing tasks being introduced. Students read, respond to an inquiry question that may or may not be "answerable" to drive their writing, and discuss their responses in Circle. As exemplified through our curricular suggestions in Chapters 1 and 3, we are committed to inclusive practices. When teachers provide reading and writing tasks in class, they ensure that everyone is involved, as opposed to focusing on who didn't do readings and written assignments in advance. If the goal is to make sure students are able to learn specific skills, then our work is to make sure they have opportunities to practice in a community.

Read Write Think Circle Examples

Read Write Think Circles are learning spaces that use the tools of restorative justice Circle processes (described in Chapter 2) to cultivate a community of readers, writers, and thinkers. Read Write Think Circles look a lot like restorative justice Community-Building Circles, including chairs placed in a circle (remember, there should never be anything in the middle of the circle except the centerpiece, and students should be encouraged to move their book bags and backpacks out of the way); a talking piece that will be used to signal that the person holding it is speaking while everyone else has an opportunity to listen (you should invite students to bring in small objects that can serve as talking pieces and represent personal stories they can share); and a centerpiece in the middle of the circle (this will help students who are struggling with sitting still by giving them something to focus their eyes on; Maisha often places books on the centerpiece that are related to the topic). Read Write Think Circles serve as prewriting activities during which students can read aloud, discuss, and write in response to a short article, poem, or excerpt related to the unit, theme, or learning objective. Initially, teachers will serve as facilitators and generate questions for "rounds," during which everyone has an opportunity to respond to the question. Ideally, students will learn how to generate questions and facilitate these Circles. The following examples are Read Write Think Circles using short op-eds, magazine articles, and documentaries—but they could easily be adapted to many kinds of reading, writing, and visual images.

Read Write Think Circle 1

Reading: "The Pain of the Watermelon Joke" by Jacqueline Woodson

Who? What? Where? Award-winning young adult literature author Jacqueline Woodson received the National Book Award in 2014 for her memoir, *Brown Girl Dreaming*. During the award ceremony, the master of ceremonies—whom Woodson considered to be a friend—joked about Woodson being allergic to watermelon, a thoughtless nod to the stereotype that all Black people enjoy watermelon. This op-ed is Woodson's response to this tasteless joke and the pain it caused at what should have been a joyous event.

Questions (to be asked in Circle prior to writing):
- What is humor? What is the purpose of humor?
- When has a joke gone too far?

- Are there stereotypes about your race/ethnicity, class, or gender that you have experienced as harmful? Why?
- Write an op-ed (appx. 400–1,200 words) about your experience, with the goal of educating an audience about why this particular stereotype is harmful. If you find that you need to conduct more research to provide a more coherent context, write about what it is you need to learn or know to generate the most effective piece of writing. (Think: What did Woodson have to learn or know about watermelon and the history of Jim Crow and Black oppression to write her piece?) Where can you conduct this research?

Extension for writing:
Woodson is the author of several young adult books. The book that won the National Book Award, *Brown Girl Dreaming*, is a memoir written as a series of poems. We advocate using the poems in this text as scaffolds for students to create their own memoirs in the form of a series of poems. These can be shared in Circle throughout the year, culminating in an edited volume the class publishes and shares with their families and other adults in the school building. Woodson also hosts a resourceful website (http://www.jacquelinewoodson.com/all-about-me/teachers/) with materials for readers, teachers, and caregivers with suggestions for how to engage with the site and get the most out of it.

Read Write Think Circle 2

Reading: "Your Cells. Their Research. Your Permission?" by Rebecca Skloot

Who? What? Where? Skloot is the author of the critically acclaimed *The Immortal Life of Henrietta Lacks*, which details how the cells of a working-poor African American woman, Henrietta Lacks, were harvested and used—without her permission or the permission of her family—to advance cancer research. In this piece, Skloot raises questions about the relationship between ethics and research.

Questions for rounds and writing:
- What is the purpose of research? Who is research for?
- What is confidentiality and what role does it play in science? Who should science research serve?
- Distribute information about the Common Rule for human subjects as it relates to different kinds of research and ask students to work in groups of no more than three to read and discuss. Come back to the Circle and discuss as a group: Is the Common Rule enough to ensure ethical behavior in human subject research? If not, what more is needed?

Extension for writing:

In addition to Skloot's first edition of *The Immortal Life of Henrietta Lacks*, she provided a Young Reader's Edition that includes a reader's guide. Most recently, HBO released a film based on the book. Like Woodson, Skloot has an extensive website and one that is dedicated to the book, including a teacher's guide, time-line, and character list (see http://rebeccaskloot.com/the-immortal-life/teaching/). The teacher's guide discusses Skloot's ability to *show* rather than *tell* the story of Henrietta Lacks. We suggest giving students an opportunity to show rather than tell stories through their own writing and using the Circle as a way to build capac-ity for such writing. This can be scaffolded by asking students to identify passages from Skloot's text with rich detail and description, and inviting students to craft their own descriptive passages (What did this experience look like? Sound like? Feel like?).

⌣

Read Write Think Circle 3

Reading: Various articles from *National Geographic*'s Special Issue: Gender Revolution.

Who? What? Where? *National Geographic* assembled a special issue titled "Gen-der Revolution" seeking to complicate the notion of gender and offer critical and nuanced vocabularies for gender identities. Complete with stories from throughout the world, as well as scientific knowledge around gender, this issue is a starting place for educators interested in exploring the topic with students. *National Geo-graphic* also created a teaching guide that includes questions for "Understanding Yourself to Understand Gender." All of the questions in this section can be used for Circle rounds and then expanded in writing prompts after Circle. This guide, available online at (http://media.nationalgeographic.org/assets/file/Gender Revolution_Guide.pdf), features stories, questions for reflection, and ways to talk to families and engage with the community.

Questions for rounds and writing:
- Why gender? Why now?
- What are *your* gender pronouns? What are your earliest memories of under-standing gender?

Extensions for writing:
- What, if any, are the gender norms for your family/community/culture? How do these converge and diverge with your views of gender?

- Write about a "defining moment in your life related to gender."[13]
- Respond to Janet Mock's quote: "We have to organize. We have to build coalitions across all of these people considered 'the other.' If we all banded together and build coalitions that were truly intersectional, we would be in power. I believe in the power of the people."[14] What does intersectionality mean to you? Why is this important?

Read Write Think Circle 4

Viewing: *The T Word* documentary by Laverne Cox

Who? What? Where? Actress, activist, and public figure, Laverne Cox guides viewers through the lives of seven trans youth who are agentive in sharing their stories as trans and queer. We recommend viewing segments of the documentary with opportunities for discussions in Circle. This documentary is part of PBS's Point of View Series, which includes guides for teachers on how to use the documentaries as teaching tools.

Questions for rounds and writing (adapted from "Behind the Lens: Extended Interviews with POV" and "Introducing Documentaries to Your Students":

1. What does *represent* mean to you?
2. What does *re-present* mean to you?
3. What feeds our understanding of gender?

Extensions for writing

- Create a learning walk in the school. What messages, if any, does the school implicitly or explicitly send about gender identity? Write about this experience and prepare to share the piece of writing in Circle.
- Select two to three images in a magazine. In what ways do these images subscribe to monolithic ideas about gender? How do these images challenge monolithic ideas about gender?

Read Write Think Circle 5

Reading: "The Stories That Bind Us" by Bruce Feiler

Who? What? Where? Feiler considers the work of psychologists Marshall Duke and Robyn Fivush as his family grapples with their family identity. According to

Duke and Fivush, young people who have a strong sense of their family stories are more likely to experience success in other areas of their lives. While every student doesn't have access to a family history, we believe that students can create "oscillating narratives" of struggle and progress that become part of their identity tool kits.

Questions for rounds and writing:

- Who are you? Why are you here?
- What traditions, practices, ways of being, and ways of knowing do you value from your family?

Extensions for writing:

- In what ways can or will you extend/grow/build on family traditions and practices? What can and will you pass on to the next generations in your family? What will you trouble and complicate?
- Compose a family story of resilience that you can and will share with the next generations.

Start Where You Are

In his groundbreaking text, *Start Where You Are, but Don't Stay There: Understanding Diversity, Opportunity Gaps, and Teaching in Today's Classrooms,* Milner (2010) offers an explanatory framework for understanding the range of opportunities—and missed opportunities—for teachers to teach and youth to learn. Five interconnected areas make up Milner's framework (pp. 13–14), including:

- Rejection of color blindness;
- Ability and skill to understand, work through, and transcend cultural conflicts;
- Ability to understand how meritocracy operates;
- Ability to recognize and shift low expectations and deficit mind-sets; and
- Rejection of context-neutral mind-sets and practices.

Milner has an encouraging message for teachers—start where you are! But he also challenges educators—don't stay there! In this spirit, we offer rubrics for teachers, grade-level teams, and school communities to self-assess where they are in the process of holistically implementing restorative justice. We offer the three frameworks in Figures 5.1 through 5.3 because we see them as nested and interdependent opportunities for the individual classroom, teaching teachers across disciplines and entire school communities. If you look across these rubrics, you'll see that restorative justice tier 1—Building and Strengthening Relationships—training is essential to beginning this work. No book, including this one, can take the place of training with an experienced facilitator. We are hearing from some teachers and administrators that restorative justice doesn't work; however, when we ask, "Have you been trained in restorative justice processes?," there is often silence, followed by people explaining that they heard a presentation or someone told them what to do. This is not the same as being trained as a skilled facilitator and doing the behind-the-scenes work to develop a restorative justice mindset (Winn, forthcoming). In these rubrics, "Mature Implementation" is about creating a culture in which students know what to expect. By "Advanced Implementation," students are able to facilitate or co-facilitate Building-Community Circles and Read Write Think Circles using classroom material. We offer these rubrics to school communities to underscore that it's okay to start where they are—with the invitation to not remain in that place.

Figure 5.1. Rubric for teachers.

Not Yet Underway	Beginning Implementation	Mature Implementation	Advanced Implementation
Restorative justice is being discussed in the school community, and school leadership is making a commitment to provide training for teachers and classified staff.	Restorative justice tier 1 community-building training completed. Welcome Circle implemented into first day or week of class. Pedagogy is beginning to be considered as part of a restorative approach.	Restorative justice tier 1 community-building and tier 2 restorative discipline training completed. Students meet in Circle weekly for checking in and for some instruction. Teacher is working toward demonstrably "calling in" all students via pedagogical avenues.	Restorative justice tier 1 community-building, tier 2 restorative discipline, and tier 3 reentry training completed. Content is shared in Circle 2–3 times a week in the form of Read Write Think Circles. Students bring in related material to use in Read Write Think Circles and can co-facilitate. Pedagogy "calls in" students and actively reflects to ensure all members (including the teacher) are constantly growing in community.

Figure 5.2. Rubric for content area or grade-level teams.

Not Yet Underway	Beginning Implementation	Mature Implementation	Advanced Implementation
Restorative justice is being discussed by content area teams or grade-level teams.	Restorative justice tier 1 community-building training completed. Teams agreed on implementing Welcome Circles first day of first week back in school in the fall and after winter break.	Restorative justice tier 1 community-building and tier 2 restorative discipline training completed. Teachers are co-planning for Circles. Teams agreed to facilitating weekly Circles for checking in and for some instruction.	Restorative justice tier 1 community-building, tier 2 restorative discipline, and tier 3 reentry training completed. Interdisciplinary content is shared in Circle 2–3 times a week in the form of Read Write Think Circles. Students bring in related material to use in Read Write Think Circles and can co-facilitate.

Figure 5.3. Rubric for school communities.

Not Yet Underway	Beginning Implementation	Mature Implementation	Advanced Implementation
Restorative justice is being discussed by school leadership, and plans are being made to train administrators, teachers, and classified staff.	Restorative justice tier 1 community-building training completed by administrators, classroom teachers, and classified staff. All classrooms implement Welcome Circles on first day of first week back in school in the fall and after winter break.	Restorative justice tier 1 community-building and tier 2 restorative discipline training completed by administrators, classroom teachers, and classified staff. School community agrees to implement Circles twice a week for new material.	Restorative justice tier 1 community-building, tier 2 restorative discipline, and tier 3 reentry training completed by administrators, classroom teachers, and classified staff. Circles are being used weekly in all classrooms for building relationships, introducing new materials, and community Read Write Think experiences.

While we could have referenced many other incidents and events that occurred during the writing process of this book that have impacted our thinking and affirmed why we believe this work must be done, we keep returning to the idea that the ELA classroom is one of the most appropriate opportunities to develop a restorative, transformative, justice-seeking community where we take a pedagogical stance to disrupt inequities in literacy instruction and overcome opportunity gaps in providing critical literacy experiences for all children. This begins with the core belief that all children deserve to have access to these skills, and that it is the responsibility of writing teachers to use their curricular powers to facilitate dialogue, cultivate purpose, and build a culture of belonging.

Appendix 1

Sample Prompting Questions and Topics for Circles

Please note: It is always important to carefully select the questions or topics to pose to the group based on the needs of the group. Always strongly consider the health of each member of the Circle. Be prepared by understanding that some of the Circle prompts may bring up a lot of emotions for Circle members.

Getting Acquainted

- Share a happy childhood memory.
- If you could be a superhero, what super powers would you choose and why?
- How would your best friend describe you?
- What would you not want to change about your life?
- If you could talk to someone from your family who is no longer alive, who would it be and why?
- If you had an unexpected free day, what would you like to do?
- If you were an animal, what animal would you be and why?
- Name two things or people who always make you laugh.
- I like to collect . . .
- If you could have a face-to-face conversation with anyone, who would it be and why?
- Describe your ideal job.
- Describe your favorite vacation.
- If you could change anything about yourself, what would it be and why?

Exploring Values

- Imagine you are in conflict with a person who is important in your life. What values do you want to guide your conduct as you try to work out that conflict?
- What is your passion?
- What do you keep returning to in your life?
- What touches your heart?
- What gives you hope?
- What demonstrates respect?
- What change would you like to see in your community? What can you do to promote that change?
- Describe a time when you acted on your core values even though others did not.

This material is adapted from Kristi Cole and Paul Dedinsky's packet of Restorative Justice Practices, Milwaukee Public Schools, Safe Schools/Healthy Students Initiative.

Storytelling from Our Lives to Share Who We Are and What Has Shaped Us (to build community)

Invite participants to share:

- A time when you had to let go of control
- A time when you were outside of your comfort zone
- An experience in your life when you "made lemonade out of lemons"
- An experience of transformation when, out of a crisis or difficulty, you discovered a gift in your life
- An experience of causing harm to someone and then dealing with it in a way you felt good about
- An experience of letting go of anger or resentment
- A time when you were in conflict with your parents or a caregiver
- An experience when you discovered that someone was very different from the negative assumptions you first made about that person
- An experience of feeling that you did not fit in

Relating to Curriculum

Invite participants to share:

- The best/worst thing about this project is . . .
- The main character in the book we are reading is like/not like me when . . .
- This topic makes me feel . . .

Appendix 2

Asking Powerful Questions

Questions for Focusing Attention

- What question, if answered, could make the most difference to the future of [our/your situation]?

- What's important to you about [our/your situation] and why do you care?

- What draws you/us to this inquiry?

- What's our intention here? What's the deeper purpose that is really worthy of our best effort?

- What opportunities can you see in [our/your situation]?

- What do we know so far/still need to learn about [our/your situation]?

- What are the dilemmas/opportunities in [our/your situation]?

- What assumptions do we need to test or challenge here in thinking about [our/your situation]?

- What would someone who had a very different set of beliefs than we do say about [our/your situation]?

Questions for Connecting Ideas and Finding Deeper Insight

- What's taking shape? What are you hearing underneath the variety of opinions being expressed?

- What's emerging here for you? What new connections are you making?

- What had real meaning for you from what you've heard? What surprised you? What challenged you?

- What's missing from this picture so far? What is it we're not seeing? What needs more clarity?

- What's been your/our major learning, insight, or discovery so far?

- What's the next level of thinking we need to do?

- If there was one thing that hasn't yet been said to reach a deeper level of understanding/clarity, what would it be?

Questions That Create Forward Movement

- What would it take to create change on this issue?

- What could make you/us feel fully engaged and energized about [our/your situation]?

Adapted from *The Art of Powerful Questions: Catalyzing Insight, Innovation and Action* by Eric E. Vogt, Juanita Brown, and David Isaacs (Mill Valley, CA: Whole Systems Associates, 2003).

- What's possible here and who cares? (Rather than "What's wrong here and who's responsible?")
- What needs our immediate attention going forward?
- If our success was completely guaranteed, what bold steps might we choose?
- What challenges might come our way and how might we meet them?
- What conversation, if begun today, could ripple out in a way that created new possibilities for the future?
- How can we support each other in taking the next steps? What unique contribution can we each make?
- What seed might we plant together today that could make the most difference to the future of [our/your situation]?

Appendix 3

Community-Building Circle Prep Sheet

Use the Community-Building Circle Preparation Guide Sheet (Appendix 4) to plan each of your Circles:

1. Welcome:

2. Purpose:

3. Introduce and Agree to Guidelines:

4. Introduction and Check-In of Participants:

5. Opening:

6. Explain Center:

7. Explain Talking Piece:

8. Storytelling Round:

9. Create Values:

10. Reminder about Guidelines:

11. Community Activity 1:

12. Community Activity 2:

13. Checkout Round:

14. Closing:

Appendix 4

Community-Building Circle Preparation Guide

Below are things to consider when using the Circle prep sheet (Appendix 3):

1. **Welcome:** In your own words and style, welcome everyone to the Circle. Thank them for coming. Express appreciation for their willingness to participate in this Community-Building Circle.

2. **Purpose:** Remind participants of the purpose of the Circle.

3. **Guidelines:** Invite participants to listen as you read the core guidelines, and add to it if they want to do so; then ask them if they agree to hold these guidelines. The Circle Keeper says something like: "Before we begin the discussion in Circle, we want to make sure that we can adhere to a few guidelines for our sharing. Please listen to these and we will discuss them. The Circle guidelines are: respect the talking piece, speak from your heart, listen with your heart, speak with respect, listen with respect, remain in the Circle, and honor privacy."

   Under "honor privacy," given that many of our classroom Circle participants are under the age of eighteen, the Circle Keeper must note that:

   - "As adults in schools, we are mandated reporters, which means that if anyone shares about harming yourself or others, experiencing abuse—physical, mental, emotional, or sexual—we will have to get help for you, and that may mean that we will have to call someone and talk with them about what was shared.

   - We don't speak about people and their stories with anyone who isn't a participant in the Circle.

   - If I shared about something (like my problem at home with my child), you will not bring the subject up to me outside of Circle— say, if you see me shopping at the local grocery store—because that is a different setting and context."

   The guidelines of the Circle are the agreements that participants make with one another about how to behave in the Circle. They establish clear expectations and common ground to provide a space where people feel safe to speak in their authentic voice, connect to others in a good way, and ensure a space that is respectful for all.

   Pass the talking piece and ask participants to name one agreement that is important to their participation in Circle (e.g., "Speak only for yourself" or "Keep body language respectful"). Write down the suggested guidelines on a sheet of paper or flip chart. When the talking piece has gone all the way around, read the list. Pass the talking piece and ask participants to indicate whether they accept these guidelines. If there are objections, explore the objections and the original purpose of the person who proposed that guideline, and then work to find wording that is acceptable to everyone.

4. **Introductions and check-in:** Invite every person to say their name and how they are feeling today.

5. **Opening:** Openings mark the time and space of the Circle as a place apart from the pace and tone of everyday life. The opening ceremony is designed to help participants center themselves, clear negative energies, encourage optimism, and honor the presence of everyone there. Lead the group in whatever opening ceremony you have chosen.

6. **Explain the centerpiece:** There is a focal point in the center of the Circle. This space usually includes a piece of fabric upon which there may be a living thing such as a plant or flowers. In traditional cultures, out of which Circle practice is drawn, representations of the four elements of air, water, earth, and fire are often present or symbolized at this center. Also included might be other special objects contributed by participants as each person is invited to place an item there that represents or says something about them. As the Circle continues, the center(piece) will begin to collect various symbols that represent the process of the community sitting around in the circle.

7. **Explain the talking piece:** Explain that the talking piece is a critical element of creating a space in which all participants can both speak and listen from a deep place of truth. The person holding the talking piece has the opportunity to speak without interruption while everyone else has the opportunity to listen without the need to respond. The talking piece will be passed around the circle from person to person. Only the person holding the talking piece may speak. It's always okay to pass the talking piece without speaking. The Circle Keeper may speak without the talking piece if necessary to facilitate the process, but generally will not speak without the talking piece. If the talking piece has a particular meaning, explain that.

8. **Storytelling round:** Tell participants that you are going to pass the talking piece around and invite them to say more about themselves if they aren't already acquainted. We recommend that the Circle Keeper share first. People will most likely model their response after the Keeper. Be authentic. Pass the talking piece and ask, "Is there anything you feel is important for us to know about how you are doing?" Sometimes it's useful to pose a question in this round that invites sharing about oneself so participants get to know one another better.

9. **Values:** To draw out collective values of the group, use one of the values exercises from one of the resource books such as *Circle Forward*, or create your own. You might:

   a. Pass out some 8" x 11" card stock. Fold the card in half. On the side facing you, write down a value you are bringing to this Circle, and on the other side write a value you are asking the others to bring to the Circle.

   b. Ask each person to say what they have written. Pass the talking piece.

   c. Ask participants if they can hold the values requested of them. Pass the talking piece.

10. **Guidelines:** Remind participants of the guidelines they agreed to at the beginning of the Circle.

11. **Community activity 1:** This can be an interactive activity, art project, discussion about a particular topic, group challenge, or sharing of stories that, as a result, moves the group to more deeply knowing one another. To draw out the community-building aspect of the activity, it's helpful to debrief after each activity.

12. **Community activity 2:** A second activity may be needed if, for example, the group needs to establish agreements when the initial discussion was about an issue.

13. **Check-out round:** Pass around the talking piece and ask participants to share their thoughts about the Circle process, or one word that sums up how they are feeling right now as the Circle comes to a close. This round encourages participants to wrap up the Circle rather than falling back into discussion.

14. **Closing:** Closings acknowledge the efforts of the Circle, affirm the interconnectedness of those present, convey a sense of hope for the future, and prepare participants to return to the ordinary space of their lives. Openings and closings are designed to fit the nature of the particular group and provide opportunities for cultural responsiveness. In an ongoing group, participants may be involved in the openings and closings or may actually design the opening and closing for the group.

Notes

1. See Glaze, Jeff. (June 23, 2016). "Outrage grows over forceful arrest of Black woman; Madison police reviewing incident." *Wisconsin State Journal*: http://host.madison.com/wsj/news/local/crime-and-courts/outrage-grows-over-forceful-arrest-of-black-woman-madison-police/article_08dfc5de-1fd6-543e-b8e5-020e35c487c4.html

2. See Bloom, J., Fausset, R., and McPhate, M. (July 17, 2016). "Baton Rouge Shooting Jolts a Nation on the Edge." *New York Times*: http://www.nytimes.com/2016/07/18/us/baton-rouge-shooting.html?_r=0

3. Our colleague, sujatha baliga, purposefully spells her name in lowercase letters.

4. In earlier work, Maisha refers to this work as a "restorative English education"; however, as her work in the area continued, she realized that "justice" must always remain intact and a part of the restorative justice discourse. Fahima Ife, one of Maisha's graduate students at the University of Wisconsin–Madison and now an assistant professor at Louisiana State University, and Adam Musser, Maisha's graduate student at the University of California, Davis, were instrumental in carrying this work forward.

5. The Children's Defense Fund released data in 2014 about the number of children who were hit on average in public schools from 2009 to 2010. Alabama, Arizona, Arkansas, Colorado, Florida, Georgia, Idaho, Indiana, Kansas, Kentucky, Louisiana, Mississippi, Missouri, North Carolina, Oklahoma, South Carolina, Tennessee, Texas, and Wyoming continue to allow corporal punishment.

6. Please research restorative justice training opportunities in your region and city. Practitioners will often be familiar with the sociopolitical context. You may also see the annotated bibliography at the end of this book for a partial list of recommended trainers.

7. We use the term *minoritized* to highlight the *active* way particular communities are labeled as "minorities," even if such communities make up the majority of an area or space. The term *minoritized* is an important reminder that deviance from the "norm" (Whiteness) is stigmatizing and encoded in language.

8. As mentioned earlier, although we introduce in this book the generalities surrounding these practices, the specifics are best learned though RJE training, a two- to three-day process that demonstrates the complex skills needed to truly facilitate this work.

9. See Appendixes 1 and 2 for further examples of prompting or guiding questions for Circles.

10. We recommend that all schools obtain a copy of *Circle Forward* by Boyes-Watson and Pranis (2015). It offers thirteen modules with complete Circles, from "Establish a Circle Practice" to "Teaching and Learning in Circle" to "Important but Difficult Conversations."

11. See the NCTE *Resolution on the Need for Diverse Children's and Young Adult Books* at http://www.ncte.org/positions/statements/diverse-books.

12. Note: If you have already given your students the Student Survey: Our Class (found on pp. 80–81), their responses might also inspire you.

13. In the *National Geographic*'s Special Issue on "Gender Revolution," Gloria Steinem and Sheryl Sandberg ask "3 Questions" for readers to consider, and this is one that we believe is central to this conversation.

14. See Mattie Khan's (December 5, 2016) "Janet Mock Is Here to Remind You Activism Doesn't Just Happen Every Four Years" in *ELLE* magazine. Retrieved from https://www.elle.com/culture/movies-tv/news/a41218/janet-mock-trans-list-interview/.

Annotated Bibliography

Where to Get Trained

Chicago, Illinois

Community Justice for Youth Institute (CJYI)
http://cjyiorg.publishpath.com/

CJYI is a beacon for youth and educators in Chicago, with an open door policy that provides support in the form of Circles to all community members. This organization operates in the true spirit of what it means to be restorative and transformative.

Umoja Student Development Corporation
http://www.umojacorporation.org/

Umoja Student Development Corporation's mission is to "equip young people to succeed in college and confidently claim their future," attaining this through partnerships with schools, communities, and families. Umoja hosts workshops focused on restorative justice, social-emotional learning (SEL) principles, and postsecondary readiness. Their website also offers excellent resources (we reference their post-election Circles in Chapter 5).

Denver, Colorado

Restorative Justice Partnership (RJP)
http://denverrp.org

The Denver School District–based Restorative Justice Partnership is a coalition of racial justice, education, labor, and community groups working to ensure widespread and high-quality implementation of restorative practices (RP) both in Denver and across the country. RJP is dedicated to ending the school-to-prison pipeline that is perpetuated by zero-tolerance policies and exclusionary discipline practices such as suspensions, expulsions, and the use of police in schools. RJP is a coalition that includes Advancement Project, Denver Classroom Teachers Association, Denver Public Schools, National Education Association, and Padres & Jóvenes Unidos.

Harrisonburg, Virginia

The Center for Justice and Peacebuilding (CJP)
https://emu.edu/cjp/

CJP, located at Eastern Mennonite University, comprises the Graduate Program in Conflict Transformation as well as the Practice and Training Institute, which houses the Summer Peacebuilding Institute, Strategies for Trauma Awareness and Resilience (STAR), and other intensive training, program, and partnership opportunities.

Zehr Institute for Restorative Justice
http://zehr-institute.org

The Zehr Institute of Restorative Justice is a program of Eastern Mennonite University's Center for Justice and Peacebuilding. Howard Zehr is now director emeritus; under the codirectorship of Carl Stauffer and Johonna Turner, the institute offers webinars, events, and online courses.

Madison, Wisconsin

YWCA Madison
https://www.ywcamadison.org/what-were-doing/restorative-justice/

Madison Metropolitan School District has partnered with the Restorative Justice Program at YWCA to train students as Circle Keepers and has its own curriculum guide for working with students in secondary settings. YWCA Madison was one of the first organizations to receive funding from a school district to train students as RJ Circle Keepers. See their video at https://www.youtube.com/watch?v=ODR1YDJgUrM.

New York City

Morningside Center for Teaching Social Responsibility
http://www.morningsidecenter.org/

The Morningside Center works with schools and teachers to build students' social and emotional skills, strengthen classroom and school communities, and use restorative practices to make schools more caring and equitable.

Northern California

CircleUp Education
https://www.circleuped.org/about-us

Founded by Tyrone Botelho and Tiffany Hoang, CircleUp Education focuses on curriculum design and training facilitation solutions. The organization refers to itself as a "social enterprise" that is "driven by producing equitable social and cultural change in our community."

Restorative Justice for Oakland Youth (RJOY)
http://rjoyoakland.org/about/

Civil rights attorney Fania E. Davis, community leader Aeeshah Clottey, and former Oakland City Council member Nancy Nadel, with a small City of Oakland Measure Y grant, founded RJOY in 2005. Currently, RJOY promotes institutional shifts toward restorative approaches that engage families, communities, and systems to repair harm and prevent reoffending. RJOY provides education, training, and technical assistance and collaboratively launches demonstration programs with school, community, juvenile justice, and research partners. Although the entire RJOY site is a wonderful resource, we highly recommend the videos (http://rjoyoakland.org/videos/), which allow you to see restorative justice in practice.

Restorative Justice Training Institute (RJTI)
http://www.rjtica.org

Rita Renjitham Alfred founded RJTI in the Bay Area in 2011 and has trained more than 4,000 educators—both classified and certified staff members—in the past six years. RJTI provides building-community and repairing relationships training (Maisha highly recommends following the former with the latter and credits Rita for strengthening her practice!).

Transformative Justice in Education (TJE) Center
https://education.ucdavis.edu/TJE

Maisha T. Winn and her partner, Lawrence "Torry" Winn, co-founded and co-direct the Transformative Justice in Education Center, which is housed in the School of Education at the University of California, Davis. TJE is a community-university collaborative committed to justice-seeking research and practice. TJE provides training and support for educators—both preservice and inservice—in integrating restorative justice discourses into curriculum across disciplines. TJE also offers Circle Keeper facilitation of topic Circles about race.

Roseville, Minnesota

Minnesota Department of Education (MDE)
https://education.mn.gov/MDE/dse/safe/clim/prac/

The MDE's unit on safe and healthy learners provides information and technical assistance regarding implementation of restorative measures in school settings. Nancy Riestenberg is the School Safety Center restorative practices specialist at the MDE and leads restorative measures for the state. She provides technical assistance on violence and bullying prevention, school connectedness, dropout prevention, cultural relevance of prevention education, crisis prevention, and recovery and restorative measures. She has provided technical assistance to the Minnesota school districts that experienced school shooting incidents.

Vancouver, British Columbia

The Centre for Restorative Justice (CRJ)
http://www.sfu.ca/crj.html

CRJ is an initiative of the Simon Fraser University School of Criminology and is viewed worldwide as having the experts in the field of violent-offence (post-incarceration) mediation. It has also been on the leading edge of adopting the Aboriginal concept of Circle remedies. For general or restorative justice in schools inquiries, please contact Dr. Brenda Morrison: brendam@sfu.ca

Books and Other Resources

Little Book Series

We highly recommend the entire library of "little books" published by Good Books. These are short and sweet with a lot of great information. Here's just a sampling of relevant titles:

- *The Little Book of Restorative Justice in Education*
- *The Little Book of Transformative Community Conferencing*
- *The Little Book of Circle Processes*
- *The Little Book of Family Group Conferences: New Zealand Style*

Maisha T. Winn
Justice on Both Sides: Transforming Education through Restorative Justice
Cambridge, MA: Harvard Education Press, 2018

This book offers four pedagogical stances for making the paradigm shift from punitive practices to a restorative justice mindset.

Living Justice Press
http://www.livingjusticepress.org/

The Living Justice Press is an incredible resource not only for books but also for lists of trainers/ trainings, videos, articles, and other resources. We cannot say enough about this press and highly recommend one of its books, *Circle Forward* by Carolyn Boyes-Watson and Kay Pranic, which has protocols, sample Circle openings and closings, and foundational information for setting up a Circle.

Resource Guides

All of these resource guides are useful in helping schools and districts imagine what restorative justice work can look like on a large scale:

- Oakland Unified School District Restorative Justice Implementation Guide: A Whole School Approach: http://rjoyoakland.org/wp-content/uploads/OUSDRJOY-Implementation-Guide.pdf
- San Francisco Unified School District Restorative Practices Whole-School Implementation Guide: http://www.healthiersf.org/Restorative Practices/Resources/documents/SFUSD%20 Whole%20School%20Implementation%20 Guide%20final.pdf
- YWCA, Madison, Wisconsin https://www.ywcamadison.org/what-were-doing/restorative-justice/restorative-justice-resources/

References

ACES Too High. (n.d.). ACEs Science 101. Retrieved from https://acestoohigh.com/aces-101/

Adichie C. N. (2009). *The danger of a single story*. TED Talk. Retrieved from https://www.ted.com/talks/chimamanda_adichie_the_danger_of_a_single_story/transcript?language=en

Alexander, M. (2010). *The new Jim Crow: Mass incarceration in the age of colorblindness*. New York: New Press.

Alexander, R. (2008). *Towards dialogic teaching: Rethinking classroom talk*. Thirsk, UK: Dialogos.

Alim, H. Samy (2016). Introducing raciolinguistics: Racing language and languaging race in hyper-racial times. In H. Samy Alim, John R. Rickford, & Arnetha F. Ball (eds.), *Raciolinguistics: How language shapes our ideas about race* (pp. 1–30). New York: Oxford University Press.

American Psychological Association. (2008). Are zero tolerance policies effective in the schools? An evidentiary review and recommendations. *American Psychologist, 63*(9), 852–62.

Amstutz, L. S., & Mullet, J. H. (2005). *The little book of restorative discipline for schools: Teaching responsibility; creating caring climates*. Intercourse, PA: Good Books.

Appleman, D. (2015). *Critical encounters in secondary English: Teaching literary theory to adolescents* (3rd ed.). New York: Teachers College Press.

Aukerman, M. (2012). "Why do you say yes to Pedro, but no to me?" Toward a critical literacy of dialogic engagement. *Theory Into Practice, 51*(1), 42–48.

Aukerman, M. (2013). Rereading comprehension pedagogies: Toward a dialogic teaching ethic that honors student sensemaking. *Dialogic Pedagogy, 1,* A1–A31.

Bishop, R. S. (1990). Mirrors, windows, and sliding glass doors. *Perspectives, 6*(3), ix–xi.

Boyd, M. P., & Markarian, W. C. (2011). Dialogic teaching: Talk in service of a dialogic stance. *Language and Education, 25*(6), 515–34.

Boyes-Watson, C., & Pranis, K. (2015). *Circle forward: Building a restorative school community*. St. Paul, MN: Living Justice Press.

Braithwaite, J. (2002). *Restorative justice and responsive regulation*. Oxford: Oxford University Press.

Cameron, L., & Thorsborne, M. (2001). Restorative justice and school discipline: Mutually exclusive? In H. Strang & J. Braithwaite (eds.), *Restorative justice and civil society* (pp. 180–94). Cambridge, UK: Cambridge University Press.

Children's Defense Fund. (2016, September 13). *Child poverty in America 2015: National analysis*. Retrieved from http://www.childrensdefense.org/library/child-poverty-in-america-2015.pdf

Christensen, L. (2009). *Teaching for joy and justice. Reimagining the language arts classroom*. Milwaukee, Rethinking Schools.

Coates, T-N. (2015, October). The black family in the age of mass incarceration. *The Atlantic*. https://www.theatlantic.com/magazine/archive/2015/10/the-black-family-in-the-age-of-mass-incarceration/403246/

Collier, L. (2016, Sept.). No longer invisible: How diverse literature helps children find themselves in books, and why it matters. *The Council Chronicle*. Retrieved from http://www.ncte.org/library/NCTEFiles/Resources/Journals/CC/0261-sept2016/NoLongerInvisible.pdf

Esteban-Guitart, M., & Moll, L. C. (2014). Funds of identity: A new concept based on the funds of knowledge approach. *Culture & Psychology, 20*(1), 31–48.

Evans, K., & Vaandering, D. (2016). *The little book of restorative justice in education: Fostering responsibility, healing, and hope in schools*. New York: Good Books.

Fabelo, T., Thompson, M. D., Plotkin, M., Carmichael, D., Marchbanks, M. P. III, & Booth, E. A. (2011). *Breaking schools' rules: A statewide study of how school discipline relates to students' success and juvenile justice involvement*. New York: Council of State Governments Justice Center.

Fisher, M. T. (2004). "The song is unfinished": The new literate and literary and their institutions. *Written Communication, 21*(3), 290–312.

Fisher, M. T. (2006). Earning "dual degrees": Black bookstores as alternative knowledge spaces. *Anthropology and Education Quarterly, 37*(1), 83–99.

Fisher, M. T. (2009). *Black literate lives: Historical and contemporary perspectives.* New York: Routledge.

Freire, P. (1973). *Education for critical consciousness.* New York: Seabury Press.

Fronius, T., Persson, H., Guckenburg, S., Hurley, N., & Petrosino, A. (2016). Restorative justice in U.S. schools: A research review. San Francisco: WestEd Justice and Prevention Research Center. Retrieved from http://jprc.wested.org/wp-content/uploads/2016/02/RJ_Literature-Review_20160217.pdf

Garcia, A. (2013). *Critical foundations in young adult literature: Challenging genres.* Rotterdam, Netherlands: Sense Publishers.

Gilyard, K. (1996). *Let's flip the script: An African American discourse on language, literature, and learning.* Detroit, MI: Wayne State University Press.

González, N., Moll, L. C., & Amanti, C. (Eds.). (2005). *Funds of knowledge: Theorizing practices in households, communities, and classrooms.* Mahwah, NJ: Erlbaum.

Greene, S. (Ed.). (2008). *Literacy as a civil right: Reclaiming social justice in literacy teaching and learning.* New York: Peter Lang.

Gutiérrez, K. D. (2008a). Developing a sociocritical literacy in the third space. *Reading Research Quarterly, 43*(2), 148–64.

Gutiérrez, K. D. (2008b). Language and literacies as civil rights. In S. Greene (Ed.), *Literacy as a civil right: Reclaiming social justice in literacy research and teaching* (pp. 169–84). New York: Peter Lang.

Gutiérrez, K. D., Asato, J., Pacheco, M., Moll, L. C., Olson, K., Horng, E. L., Ruiz, R., Garcia, E., & McCarty, T. L. (2002). "Sounding American": The consequences of new reforms on English language learners. *Reading Research Quarterly, 37*(3), 328–43.

Hauschildt, T. (2012, July 15). *Gacaca courts and restorative justice in Rwanda.* E-International Relations: Students. Retrieved from http://www.e-ir.info/2012/07/15/gacaca-courts-and-restorative-justice-in-rwanda/

Johnston, P. H. (2012). *Opening minds: Using language to change lives.* Portland, ME: Stenhouse.

Juzwik, M. M., Borsheim-Black, C., Caughlan, S., & Heintz, A. (2013). *Inspiring dialogue: Talking to learn in the English classroom.* New York: Teachers College Press.

Kidde, J., & Alfred, R. R. (2011, August 18). Restorative justice: A working guide for our schools. Alameda County School Health Services Coalition. Retrieved from https://www.skidmore.edu/campusrj/documents/Kidde-and-Alfred-2011.pdf

King, Martin Luther, Jr. (2010). *Where do we go from here: Chaos or community?* Boston: Beacon Press.

Ladson-Billings, G. (1995). Toward a theory of culturally relevant pedagogy. *American Educational Research Journal, 32*(3), 465–91.

Ladson-Billings, G. (2005). Reading, writing, and race: Literacy practices of teachers in diverse classrooms. In T. L. McCarty (ed.), *Language, literacy, and power in schooling* (pp. 133–50). Mahwah, NJ: Lawrence Erlbaum.

Ladson-Billings, G. (2006). From the achievement gap to the education debt: Understanding achievement in U.S. schools. *Educational Researcher, 35*(7), 3–12.

Lee, C. D. (1998). Culturally responsive pedagogy and performance-based assessment. *The Journal of Negro Education, 67*(3), 268–79.

Lewis, C. (1993). "Give people a chance": Acknowledging social differences in reading. *Language Arts, 70*(6), 454–61.

Losen, D. J., & Orfield, G. (Eds.). (2002). *Racial inequity in special education.* Cambridge, MA: Harvard Education Press.

MaCrae, A., & Zehr, H. (2004). *The little book of family group conferences: New Zealand style.* Intercourse, PA: Good Books.

Marchetti, E., & Daly, K. (2004). Indigenous courts and justice practices in Australia. *Trends & Issues in Crime and Criminal Justice, No. 277.* Australian Institute of Criminology. Retrieved from http://www.aic.gov.au/media_library/publications/tandi_pdf/tandi277.pdf

Mascareñaz, L. (2016, Nov. 2). The day after. *Teach-*

ing Tolerance. Retrieved from https://www.toler
ance.org/magazine/the-day-after

McHenry, E., & Heath, S. B. (1994). The literate
and the literary: African Americans as writers and
readers—1830–1940. *Written Communication,
11*(4), 419–44.

Mehan, H. (1979). "What time is it, Denise?": Asking known information questions in classroom
discourse. *Theory Into Practice, 18*(4), 285–94.

Mercer, N., & Hodgkinson, S. (Eds.). (2008). *Exploring talk in schools: Inspired by the work of Douglas
Barnes.* Los Angeles: SAGE.

Milner, H. R., IV (2010). *Start where you are, but don't
stay there: Understanding diversity, opportunity gaps,
and teaching in today's classrooms.* Cambridge, MA:
Harvard Education Press.

Moll, L. C., Amanti, C., Neff, D., & Gonzalez, N.
(1992). Funds of knowledge for teaching: Using a
qualitative approach to connect homes and classrooms. *Theory Into Practice, 31*(2), 132–41.

Morgan E., Salomon, N., Plotkin, M., & Cohen, R.
(2014). *The school discipline consensus report: Strategies from the field to keep students engaged in school
and out of the juvenile justice system.* Justice Center:
The Council of State Governments. Retrieved
from https://csgjusticecenter.org/wp-content/
uploads/2014/06/The_School_Discipline_
Consensus_Report.pdf

Morrell, E., Dueñas, R., Garcia, V., & López,
J. (2013). *Critical media pedagogy: Teaching for
achievement in city schools.* New York: Teachers
College Press.

Morris, M. W. (2016). *Pushout: The criminalization of
black girls in schools.* New York: New Press.

Morrison, B. (2007). *Restoring safe school communities:
A whole school response to bullying, violence and alien-
ation.* Annandale, NSW, Aust.: Federation Press.

Morrison, B. (2012). What is restorative justice?
SFU Continuing Studies Series [Video]. Re-
trieved from https://www.youtube.com/channel/
UCUi_6IJ8IgUAzI6JczJUVPA

Noguera, P. A., Pierce, J. C., & Ahram, R. (Eds.)
(2016). *Race, equity, and education: Sixty years from
Brown.* Cham, Switz.: Springer.

Nystrand, M., with Gamoran, A., Kachur, R., &
Prendergast, C. (1997). *Opening dialogue : Under-
standing the dynamics of language and learning in the
English classroom.* New York: Teachers College
Press.

O'Connell, T. (1998, August). *From Wagga Wagga
to Minnesota.* Paper presented at the First International Conference on Conferencing, Minneapolis,
MN.

O'Reilley, M. R. (1984). *The peaceable classroom.* Col-
lege English, 46(2), 103–12.

Paris, D. (2012). Culturally sustaining pedagogy: A
needed change in stance, terminology, and practice. *Educational Researcher, 41*(3), 93–97.

Paris, D., & Alim, H. S. (Eds.). (2017). *Culturally sustaining pedagogies: Teaching and learning for justice
in a changing world.* New York: Teachers College
Press.

Phillippo, K. (2012). "You're trying to know me":
Students from nondominant groups respond to
teacher personalism. *The Urban Review, 44*(4),
441–67.

Pranis, K. (2005). *The little book of circle processes: A
new/old approach to peacemaking.* Intercourse, PA:
Good Books.

Prendergast, C. (2002). The economy of literacy:
How the Supreme Court stalled the Civil Rights
Movement. *Harvard Educational Review, 72*(2),
206–29.

Prevent Child Abuse America & KPJR Films. (2016).
The facilitator's guide to *Resilience:* A discussion
guide to accompany screenings of the documentary film. Retrieved from http://preventchildabuse
.org/wp-content/uploads/2016/09/Resilience-
Guide-FINAL.pdf

Rosenblatt, L. M. (1994). *The reader, the text, the
poem: The transactional theory of the literary work.*
Carbondale: Southern Illinois University Press.

Schultz, K. (2009). *Rethinking classroom participation:
Listening to silent voices.* New York: Teachers
College Press.

Shannon, P. (1998). *Reading poverty.* Portsmouth,
NH: Heinemann.

Staats, C. (2014, May). Implicit racial bias and school
discipline disparities: Exploring the connection.
Kirwan Institute Special Report. Retrieved from
http://kirwaninstitute.osu.edu/wp-content/
uploads/2014/05/ki-ib-argument-piece03.pdf

Staton, S. F. (1987). *Literary theories in praxis.* Philadelphia: University of Pennsylvania Press.

Sumner, M. D., Silverman, C. J., & Frampton, M. L. (2010). *School-based restorative justice as an alternative to zero-tolerance policies: Lessons from West Oakland.* Thelton E. Henderson Center for Social Justice, University of California, Berkeley, School of Law. Retrieved from https://www.law.berkeley .edu/files/thcsj/10-2010_School-based_Restora tive_Justice_As_an_Alternative_to_Zero-Tolerance_Policies.pdf

Tello, J. (2017, June). Keynote address. Sixth National Conference on Community and Restorative Justice. *Moving restorative justice from margins to center: We're the ones we've been waiting for.* Oakland, California.

Thomas, E. E., & Stornaiuolo, A. (2016). Restorying the self: Bending toward textual justice. *Harvard Educational Review, 86*(3), 313–38.

Turner, C. (2016, September 5). Preschool suspensions really happen and that's not okay with Connecticut. *National Public Radio.* Retrieved from http://www.npr.org/sections/ed/2016/09/05/ 490226345/preschool-suspensions-really-happen-and-thats-not-okay-with-connecticut

Willis, A. I. (2008). *Reading comprehension research and testing in the U.S.: Undercurrents of race, class, and power in the struggle for meaning.* New York: Lawrence Erlbaum.

Winn, M. T. (2011). *Girl time: Literacy, justice, and the school-to-prison pipeline.* New York: Teachers College Press.

Winn, M. T. (2013). Forum: Toward a restorative English education. *Research in the Teaching of English, 48*(1), 126–35.

Winn, M. T. (2016, October 28). *Agitating. Educating. Organizing. Toward a theory of black literate lives.* Race, Inequality, and Language in Education Conference, Stanford University.

Winn, M. T. (2018). *Justice on both sides: Transforming education through restorative justice.* Cambridge, MA: Harvard Education Press.

Winn, M. T., & Johnson, L. P. (2011). *Writing instruction in the culturally relevant classroom.* Urbana, IL: National Council of Teachers of English.

Worthy, J., Consalvo, A. L., Bogard, T., & Russell, K. W. (2012). Fostering academic and social growth in a primary literacy workshop classroom: "Restorying" students with negative reputations. *Elementary School Journal, 112*(4), 568–89.

Zehr, H. (2002). *The little book of restorative justice.* Intercourse, PA: Good Books.

Zehr, H. (2015). *Changing lenses: Restorative justice for our times.* Harrisonburg, VA: Herald Press.

Zemelman, S. (2016). *From inquiry to action: Civic engagement with project-based learning in all content areas.* Portsmouth, NH: Heinemann.

Index

Note: An *n* following a page number indicates a note; an *f* indicates a figure.

Authors

Rita Renjitham Alfred has dedicated many years to serving youth and families in the Bay Area. She started her career in restorative justice as the restorative justice coordinator at Cole Middle School in the Oakland [California] Unified School District (OUSD) and later with Restorative Justice for Oakland Youth. She interfaced with the various system stakeholders, including school site and district administration, teachers, students and families, school and city police, and community-based organizations, to lead a successful program. The pilot program at Cole was so effective in reducing suspensions, expulsions, and violence that staff at approximately 20 additional schools sought training and technical assistance to bring restorative practices to their sites. Due in large part to these efforts, in January 2010, Renjitham Alfred and others helped the OUSD School Board pass a resolution adopting restorative justice district-wide as official policy. Since that time, she has trained more than 4,000 people in schools, coaching and consulting with six other school districts to adopt restorative justice practices at their schools. As an independent contractor, she founded the Restorative Justice Training Institute, which holds RJ trainings and consults and coaches in schools. Renjitham Alfred collaborates with teachers to integrate RJE elements in daily academic classes. She has two sons and two grandchildren and lives in the Bay Area.

Hannah Graham is a curriculum consultant and professional development leader who works with schools and nonprofit organizations interested in enhancing classroom literacy instruction. A former secondary ELA teacher, Graham's work focuses on advancing the power of educators and their students to transform classroom communities using reading and writing as central tools. She is currently director of professional learning for WebbAlign and a PhD candidate in the Department of Curriculum and Instruction at the University of Wisconsin-Madison.

Maisha T. Winn is Chancellor's Leadership Professor at the University of California, Davis, and codirector (with Torry Winn) of UC Davis's Transformative Justice in Education (TJE) Center. Her program of research examines the ways in which teachers and/or adult allies for youth in schools and in out-of-school contexts practice "justice" in the teaching of literacy. Winn was named an American Educational Research Association Fellow in 2016, received the William T. Grant Foundation Distinguished Fellowship in 2014, and received the American Educational Research Association Early Career Award in 2012. She has authored several books, including *Writing in Rhythm: Spoken Word Poetry in Urban Schools* (2007, published under "Fisher"), *Black Literate Lives: Historical and Contemporary Perspectives* (2009, published under "Fisher"), *Girl Time: Literacy, Justice, and the School-to-Prison Pipeline* (2011), and most recently *Justice on Both Sides: Transforming Education through Restorative Justice* (2018), and is coeditor of *Humanizing Research: Decolonizing Qualitative Inquiry with Youth and Communities* (with Django Paris). Winn is also the author of numerous articles in peer-reviewed journals, including *Review of Research in Education; Anthropology and Education Quarterly; International Journal of Qualitative Studies in Education; Race Ethnicity and Education; Research in the Teaching of English; Race and Social Problems;* and *Harvard Educational Review*.

This book was typeset in Janson Text and BotonBQ by
Barbara Frazier.

Typefaces used on the cover include American Typewriter,
Frutiger, and Formata.

The book was printed on 50-lb. White Offset paper
by Seaway Printing.